DIVINE ENCOUNTERS:

THE REALITY OF GOD, ANGELS & DEMONS

By Dawn Densmore

*D*ivine *E*ncounters:

THE REALITY OF GOD, ANGELS & DEMONS

Dawn Densmore

Cover Picture by: Cindy Hale

Book Cover Design by: Tamara Smith

Scriptures are from the Holy Bible, King James Version

©Copyright 2012

ISBN 978-1-4675-5046-8

Dedicated to:

GOD

Thanks to:

My deep gratitude and thanks to those who are included in this book, as well as to those who encouraged and supported me during the process of writing with thoughtful feedback. My thanks especially to Cindy, Tami, Fabien, Nancy, Cheryl, Marti, Sue, Lynne, Becky, Patti, Polly, Treya & Ron, Lisa, April, and to my father, Gardner, who suggested I write this book.

CONTENTS

INTRODUCTION

This book contains events that have been used like stepping stones to help me understand the meaning behind life, the reality of God's presence, as well as the reality of angels and demons. God's promise is "Ye shall know the truth, and the truth shall make you free." Free to see God in very ordinary things that happen every day on earth, free to move forward not knowing the outcome of decisions, and free to focus on "God's will be done, on earth, as it is in heaven." Each day provides opportunities to experience God's mercy, grace, and love – not always through great things, but often through very small things. These experiences transform and connect us to each other and allow us to 'see' beyond the material world into a dimension where there is peace and joy and the knowledge that we belong to God. Jesus Christ promised not to leave us nor forsake us. He has promised the suffering of this present time is not worthy to be compared with the glory reserved for us. Belief in God and in the work of Jesus Christ, as a child, *is* what sets us free.

Chapter 1:

The End of Time – The Accounting

For there is nothing hid, which shall not be manifested; neither

was anything kept secret, but that it should come abroad.

Mark 4:22

It was 3 a.m. when I found myself no longer in my physical body. I was instead in a very large space that seemed to go on and on, with rows and rows of very small 'cubes' stacked side by side, for it seemed like miles. I was in one of those cubes, in one of those rows, fully aware of my being, and in a place where an accounting was going on. I watched and listened as each cube ahead of me in line, was opened, scanned and read. Each housed a 'soul' that had lived on earth and there seemed to be no end to the number of cubes in this gigantic area. Everyone was listening and hearing the 'reading' of each cube. Entire lifetimes were being processed, some within what would be on earth just seconds. I was astounded by what I, and everyone else, heard.

Each life account contained everything that had happened, good and bad, including every thought and every action that could have been taken, but was not, as well as actions that were taken and the motive behind each action. Most important of all, secrets previously totally concealed were all being disclosed, and everyone was hearing them.

As I listened to each reading, I recalled one of my friends telling me his policy of, "Lie til you die", and another friend who together with his buddy had orchestrated a 'payback' to someone who had offended him. The payback occurred one night on a drive home when three baby skunks were found huddled around their dead mother on the side of the road. He and his friend had stopped to pick up the baby skunks to keep them as pets. But once they were picked up, the baby skunks started to spray. It was then that the thought of payback had occurred.

They got a bag from the car, and hurriedly put the baby skunks into the bag and headed to that friend's home. The skunks began to stink so badly that they put the bag of skunks out the window and drove fast to minimize the terrible smell which continued to increase. Once they arrived at their friend's home, they parked far away and walked up the street with the bag of skunks and went to the cellar door. They opened the door and dropped the skunks out of the bag into the basement and closed the door. Then they ran and hid behind a tree to watch.

Soon all of the lights in the house came on, and everyone in the house came out. They watched as a search with flashlights began outside and finally they realized the odor was coming from their basement. He told me this story one night as an example of something he had done years earlier that he wished he had not done. Both of these souls were behind me in my generational row. I wondered how each of us would handle our readings.

When a cube finished being read, I could feel my cube being moved forward, closer to the place where I too, would be opened and read. There was no way for any of us to get out of our cubes or to avoid being read. There was no way for anyone to alter or change things now, each of our life's moments had already been recorded. Every second of time that we had lived on earth had been saved for this accounting.

My mind began to race and I became anxious as I remembered my life experiences. I remembered things that had happened in my life that I had completely forgotten. As lives continued to be disclosed, I thought about my own secrets that no one knew. These secrets began flashing through my mind, as well as experiences that included my own indiscretions, lies, and errors in judgment that had caused sorrow for me, as well as others. I remembered times when I had heard God's audible voice speak to me. I thought about the demons that had physically attacked me, as well as encounters I had with angels that had come to help me. All of the experiences I had kept secret would be disclosed. My mind raced, and I worked hard to gain control over how my own 'reading' would be. Thoughts of my atheist friend now flashed before me. I knew things about him too, that others did not know.

Suddenly I was back in my physical body, and back in my bedroom. The experience of being out of my body at a divine accounting was vivid in my mind. I could not shake the reality of what had just happened to me.

I thought, "So this is how 'the end of time' will begin." It was profound to realize that every single soul that had ever lived was going to have to give an account for each action and for every thought, as well as for every feeling, every pain, every sorrow, every joy, every failure, every victory – everything experienced within the course of their lifetime on earth. Everything had been recorded just like keystrokes on a computer, stored and kept for the divine accounting. All of us would be like Daniel in the Bible who was told by an angel that he would stand in his lot at the end of his days. Each of us would stand in our 'lot' and would have our own accounting of our deeds before every soul that had ever lived within a fleshly body on earth—and then eternity would begin.

I was unable to sleep as my mind worked to sort through my life, of experiences long forgotten. I remembered my miracle cat called 'Buffy', and the night I had been awakened by a 'push', the unexplained light that had appeared from nowhere in the middle of the night in my bedroom, my divine transport out of my body to the throne in heaven; and the many people who had appeared to me after they had died. My life was full of unexplainable events, unexpected twists and turns, as well as a few strategically placed trials that had tested the very core of my faith, making me feel at times, as though I were all alone.

But now, I was just excited to be back in my body and no longer in that cube where my life had been just about to be opened and read. And as my time on earth ticked away - seconds into minutes, and minutes into hours, and hours into days, and days into weeks, and weeks into months, and months into years that would never return again; right *now*, my time on earth still counted! Right now, I was relieved. God had granted me a second opportunity on earth for better choices -- better decisions and I was very grateful.

Some say 'time' heals all wounds, but some wounds are

so deep, healing cannot occur at all without divine intervention. When that happens, only a different perspective can cause a desire to get back in the game, to be willing to once again give tasks our full attention. Being out of my body and experiencing the accounting at the end of time did just that.

Chapter 2

The Atheist – Heart Work

The readings had been amazing in their depth. Each accounting had been beyond the surface appearance, beyond what people thought about other people, and of what we 'thought' people thought about us. Each soul had been examined for the motivation behind everything that had occurred. Things that had been done to gain the approval of men, even when good, lost their very appearance of value. Only one thing had mattered, and that was love.

While on earth, God had given men free will choice, and that meant that everyone had been free to do as they desired. There had not been a 'you must' or 'you shall' from God. Each soul that had lived had been allowed to exercise 'free will choice' while on earth. The tares and the wheat had grown side by side. The accounting was at the end of time, during which every soul was aware of the importance for divine forgiveness, and of the critical role of the life of Jesus Christ in that very forgiveness. Here, every soul was acknowledging their need for forgiveness. Here, things considered of little value on earth were esteemed of high value, and those things of great value were seen as worth very little.

The Two Important Things

When Jesus Christ was on earth he said there were two commandments that fulfilled the entire law: to love God with all your heart, with all your mind, and with all soul and to love your neighbor as yourself. The last instructions he gave while He was on earth were before 500 witnesses. And those instructions were to go and share the good news of eternal life for all who believe. Then, as he told everyone that he would return to set up his kingdom on earth, a cloud circled his feet and carried him up into heaven.

I had spent a lot of my time on earth, attempting to learn as much as I could about the meaning of the words written in the Bible. My mind always had questions about everything I read and I pondered and thought about those things. Many of my questions did not have answers. I had deliberately decided to not focus on what I did not understand, but I had determined within my heart to focus and do the things that I did understand. What I did understand was that God was love, and that responses of kindness and love, united me with God and with others. Living life that way was not easy.

The Atheist

I had met the man who was an atheist through a care agency that had assigned me to him to provide non-medical help. Within an hour of meeting him he asked me a direct question, "What do you believe?" I said, "You know, I am not permitted to discuss this topic on assignments; but since you asked, I will tell you. My faith is in the man that walked through walls, who appeared and disappeared; the one that rose from the dead, the one who said he would come again, and his name would be Jesus."

He leaned forward in his chair, "Do you know what people like *me* in the medical field call people like *you*?" This man was a well-known physician within the medical field and was used as an expert in trials for his extensive medical knowledge. I replied "I don't know! What **do** people 'like you' say about people 'like me' in the medical field?" He leaned further forward in his chair to place his head closer to where I was seated, and responded, "*You* are delusional!" I, too, now leaned closer forward in my chair, so that our faces locked in position within a foot of each other and replied, "I totally understand! People that have faith believe with their 'heart' not their 'head.' There is no way to understand the things of God with our minds. We are told to trust in the Lord with all our hearts and to not lean unto our own understanding, in all our ways to acknowledge him and that when we do that, he will direct our paths."

The Work Begins

My assignment was on weekends which started on a Friday night and finished on Sunday night. During the year and a half that I was with this man, he would continually attempt to engage me in intellectual conversations to entice me to defend my faith, but I refused to engage in any arguments with him. Each time I would pray as hard as I could for the Lord to soften his heart and help him to have faith. Only the Lord could melt this man's giant iceberg of unbelief.

As I continued to pray and care for him, small miracles began to occur. One day he informed me that he was unable to see out of one of his eyes. It had come upon him suddenly. He said, "I don't want to alarm you, but I am worried. You need to take me to the doctor's." Immediately I began to pray for him, "Lord his plate is pretty full right now, please don't add another thing, please spare him! If it is possible, please restore his sight!"

Before we could even get into the car to go to the hospital, he suddenly could see again out of that eye. We continued to the hospital, but the doctors found nothing wrong with his eye. He was amazed and so was I. And the loss of sight in that eye never returned.

He was required to use a walker and I shadowed him

when he walked. I had been told that sometimes he would drop to his knees and be unable to get back up. One day when I was shadowing him he did fall to his knees. Once he was on his knees, he laid down the rest of the way onto the floor, and discouragingly said, "Just call 911!" I said, "I think I can help you to get up." "Really!" he replied. "Yes, I am sure of it," I told him. He almost laughed in my face. I added, "If I can't get you up in five minutes, I will call 911."

As I surveyed the situation, I asked if he could get back onto his knees. Yes, he could do that. I asked if he could walk on his knees the short distance to the side of the bed. Yes, he could do that. Once he was next to the bed, I put a chair beside him, and a chair behind him. I had him put one hand on the chair and had him push himself up, with his other hand on the bed.

As he did so, I helped him move one leg up and asked him to put weight on that foot. As he did so, I slid the chair behind his rear and he was able to sit down. He was just amazed how easy it had been to get back up.

He looked up at me and said, "Usually I am on the floor for over an hour! I cannot believe that you got me up in just a few minutes! It takes the rescue squad forever to get here." He then said, Thank you!" and patted my hand in gratitude.

A Divine Lesson - Humility

One of my roles was to escort him to his doctor's appointments. On one trip he had a problem. He had to use the bathroom and there wasn't enough time for him to get there. I was directed to a bathroom for him to use but it was very small. Because he clearly needed my help, I went in with him. Now we were very close to each other in this very small space. I was able to get gloves and scissors from the desk and cut off his soiled underwear. I carefully removed them as he stood, and folded them together and placed them in the trash bin. I then tied the plastic bag at the top. His outer pants did not get soiled, and he was able to quickly use wads of toilet tissue to clean himself, as I flushed frequently. He was now clean, but he was worried about another accident. I asked him to wait just one minute.

I went outside and spotted a medical blue liner pad on the counter with medical supplies on top. I asked the attendant for it. She quickly removed the supplies and gave it to me. I brought it to him in the bathroom. He asked, "What are you going to do with that?" I said, "We can add it as a liner in your pants!" I quickly placed it front to back between his legs and held it in place as I instructed him to pull up his pants and belt them. As he did, I said, "You know, life is about lessons."

He asked, "And *what exactly* would this lesson be?" I replied, "This lesson would be about humility, one of the hardest virtues to acquire on earth, and it means exactly what it is called.

Our bodies are cumbersome down here. It will be wonderful when we have bodies like Jesus, that do not need all of this care! I want you to know how truly honored I am to get to help you. In truth, we are all the same in the end, no one is any better than another else." He smiled and thanked me. He met with his doctor, and we went back home without any further incident.

Even though he was a professed atheist, he had a friend who was a minister who visited him often. Whenever he visited, intellectual questions would fly in his direction, questions that had no answers, questions that were designed to generate strife rather than an acknowledgment of the possible limitations of the human mind related to creation and the universe. The minister was always patient and during each visit he would encourage his atheist friend using Bible verses to have faith.

A Hippopotamus

During the last two weeks of his life, a hospital bed was moved into his living room for him. During what I knew would be my last weekend assignment, I prayed very hard. I asked the Lord for wisdom to know what to say to him. There was really nothing I could do for him now but to pray. Suddenly I realized I had something that I could actually give him, my stuffed hippopotamus -- my comfort. I slept with that hippo every night.

In the morning before I left his home I went to him at his bedside. "I have something for you," I said as I handed him my hippo. "What *is* **this**?" he asked, as he held it up in the air. "It's comfort! It's my hippo that I have slept with every night. It is the only thing I can give you now. Would you like to pray with me?" I asked.

Quite unexpectedly, he smiled broadly and nodded and said, "Yes!" He repeated a prayer after me, "Lord Jesus I believe you died on the cross and that you rose from the dead. Please forgive me for my sins and remember me when I come into your Kingdom." I said, "I may not see you again on this earth, but I *will* see you on the other side. Please be sure to tell Jesus, I said "Hi" when you see him." He said, "I will do that!"

I left that day so happy. I missed not having my hippopotamus to sleep with but I was so glad I had given it to him. He died about a week later. I attended his funeral. His minister friend announced to everyone that he was a confirmed atheist. As the minister spoke, I cried. I knew he was in heaven. I told the Lord I wanted to let the minister know that he had prayed with me but there wasn't an opportunity to do that that day.

About a month later I met with one of his day caregivers and we talked about his last days. I shared with her how I had given him my hippo. "Is that what that was!" she exclaimed. "I have to tell you Dawn, he did not want anyone to take that hippo away from him. Whenever we moved him, or cared for him, he asked for it back." Both of us were moved emotionally that the Lord had used my hippo to provide him with some comfort in his last days on earth.

Three Years Later

Fast forward three years. I was assigned to be with a woman whose husband had just been put into an assisted living facility. She was exhausted and needed someone to make her supper. When I arrived, I prepared the meal and cleaned up. As I cleaned I noticed a picture of a man with a collar. "That is my husband," she told me. I said, "Hum, I know him, but I just can't seem to place him." We talked some more.

Before I left, I told her I was honored to be with her. I said, "I have had the privilege of being with many important people, a doctor, a lawyer, and some professors." She asked, "What doctor have you been with?" I replied, "Well, the doctor I was with has died. I can share his first name, so I told her his first name." The woman became pale, "Was it W.W.? she asked. "Indeed," I replied.

"He was my husband's best friend," she told me. Suddenly we both looked at each other. I said, "I have something important to tell you and your husband. Even though he was an atheist, he is in heaven! He prayed with me a week before he died." She replied, "Oh, I know! He appeared to my husband after he died and said, "Thank you." She asked me to visit her husband at the facility and tell him my story. I told her I would definitely go to visit her husband.

I went the very next day to see her husband who had been W.W.'s minister. When I got there, the minister was quite happy to see me. We talked and I told him how I had met his wife, and about my experience with his best friend, the atheist.

The minister's doctor entered just as this minister exclaimed to me, "He came back to me after he died you know, and said 'Thank you!' " I replied, "Your wife told me that he had appeared to you. Your visits were so important. You were one of his best friends, and it was your ability to share your faith with him that helped him to accept Christ. We are truly co-laborers together in the eternal harvest of the Lord."

As I spoke I looked at his doctor, and pulled out a tract* (*A small piece of folder paper with bible verses.) and handed it to him, "This is in memory of our friend, W.W. who is now in heaven on the other side." As I handed these to his Doctor, the minister waved his hand and said, "Hi up there, I'll be joining you soon!" The doctor looked at me. I smiled as I let go of the tracts and said, "It's great to know where you are going when you die!" He said, "Thanks!"

I had been amazed by how the Lord had worked in answer to my prayers for this man who told me he had no faith. W.W. was in heaven because of the incredible mercy and grace of the Lord and because of the many prayers that were said for him. W.W.'s soul accounting would contain a big surprise for everyone who knew him. Through him, I learned more what love is all about.

Charity suffered long and is kind, charity envieth not, charity vaunted not itself, is not puffed up, doth not behave itself unseemly, seeketh not her own, is not easily provoke, thinketh no evil, rejoiceth not in iniquity, but rejoiceth in the truth: beareth all things, believeth all things, hopeth all things, endureth all things. Charity never faileth. . . . And now abideth faith, hope, charity, these three; but the greatest of these is charity. 1 Corinthians 13: 4-8

Chapter 3

The Pivotal Decision - God's Voice

I continued to remember more and more events that I knew would be included in my accounting. I remembered things from when I was very young that I had long forgotten, including my first experience of God's intervention in my life. The entire experience rushed back into my mind in vivid detail.

God's Voice

I was five years old. There was no way to know how one decision at that age would impact my entire life. But through that one decision I had heard God speak directly to me. And that one decision occurred over something that was of great value to me.

At four years old, one of my joys was dolls. When the Sears catalog arrived, I could hardly wait to open it to the doll section. I spent hours looking at pictures of dolls. Once I had selected my favorite, I carried the catalog to my Mom and said,

"This is the 'doll' I want!"

"Well, that *is* a very fancy doll," she replied. "How about I get you a baby doll?" "Baby dolls are nice, but I want a grown up doll!" I replied.

We lived on a dairy farm in Vermont, and I was one of six girls. Our family would continue to grow into eight girls and one boy. My very wise Mom never gave me a grown up doll. Instead she gave me a children's book called, "Ukulele's Doll." It was a story about a little girl who was given two dolls - - a very beautiful doll and a baby doll. In the story, the little girl came to the conclusion that the baby doll was better and more fun because it could be played with without being destroyed. The book became my favorite and I read it over and over. I did enjoy playing with my baby doll more after reading that children's book, but I still desired a beautifully dressed doll.

One thing leads to another

One Christmas our Dad put six baby cradles under the Christmas tree and a baby carriage. That made playing with my baby doll even more exciting. Now I could take her for a ride and put her to bed. As I played, I realized she needed clothes. She only had pajamas to wear.

My mother had an old sewing machine that she used to mend clothes. Surely, I thought, my Mom can make a dress for my baby doll. The next time my Mom went to use the sewing machine, I was right behind her. "Mom, please make a dress for my baby doll!" I begged. My Mom looked at me and at the baby doll in my hand. "Well, I don't have time to make her anything today," she replied.

My Mom did not have time in the days that followed either, but a new ritual had begun. Whenever she was at the sewing machine, I was at her feet with my doll, and I would wait each time for her to make clothes for me. But months went by and I had no dress for my doll. Nonetheless, I was determined and tried not to get discouraged. I prayed to God, "Please, God help my Mom to have time to make a dress for my doll."

One day, before she even sat down to sew, she said, "Let

me see your baby doll." She took the doll and looked at it. She had no dress pattern to follow. I watched as she began to cut out fabric and then sew the pieces together into a doll dress. The dress fit my doll almost perfectly. I know, now, that my Mom had no idea how to make something from nothing -- but my persistence had won her heart to at least try, and she succeeded!

The Threat

The next summer I began taking my doll for rides in the baby carriage in our driveway. Our driveway went around the house and up to the barn. My older sisters had turned into 'tomboys' and had begun to pick on me, calling me 'city girl.' I inherited their dolls because they no longer played with them. They began to make fun of me. One day, one of them took my doll, held her up in the air, and threatened to tear her clothes off and drop her on the ground. They were older and enjoyed threatening me. To me, my doll *was* in real danger.

To avoid them and to protect my doll, I began to use only the lower section of the driveway for my trips with the baby carriage. In that location, I went unnoticed. I could go back and forth between the main road and the corner of the house with less fear. Soon, however, I felt constrained by the restricted space. The whole driveway was four times as long and much more fun and I longed to use it again.

As I went back and forth, I thought, 'If I go around the corner, they will see me for sure and they will take my doll and do all they said they would!' But I became determined to go around the corner. I would fight. I would protect my doll. I would not let them hurt her even if it meant I might be hurt. As I mustered the courage, I prayed and asked God to help me. I pushed my baby carriage willfully around the corner.

To my utter amazement, as I turned the corner, absolutely no one was there! I stood in the driveway shocked by the reality that I did not have to fight at all! I had been fearful of something that did not happen. I stood in the driveway, stunned.

Suddenly I heard a voice say, *"Play with your dolls, Dawn, you will not always be able to play with your dolls."* I looked around to see who had spoken to me. There was no one there. I was all alone. I definitely heard a male voice of authority and the voice had spoken directly to me and had used my name. I wondered about the voice. Where did it come from? Who was it? But there were no answers.

A Pivotal Decision

I determined it must have been God who had spoken to me and that I must obey and play with my doll! I played as hard as I could that day. I made dozens of trips up and down the entire driveway with my doll carriage with an added sense of divine protection. Hearing God's voice had removed my fear and empowered me with courage.

That unusual outcome at five years old had empowered me throughout my life to pray and to be willing to walk by faith. Whenever I would encounter fearful situations, I would remember that corner, and pray for courage to move forward.

Eighteen years would pass before I would hear what I had determined to be God's voice again.

My sisters as adults had apologized many times for picking on me when I was young. I, too, had explained to them how blessed I was by those very experiences for they had made me strong.

And we know that all things work together for good to them that love God, to them who are the called according to his purpose. Romans 8:28

Chapter 4

Harden not your Heart - Another Voice

I had seen in the accounting how motives mattered. My search for the meaning of life had taken me down a very dangerous road. After I had heard God's voice, I longed to hear Him again. When I got old enough, I was allowed to go to church on Sundays. The outside and the inside of the church filled me with wonder and amazement. Surely in this place I would hear God speak to me again. But in spite of the all of the majestic displays, the mysterious smells, the stained glass windows, the statues, and the ceremony of it all, I heard nothing. I did not understand any of it.

At Six Years Old

My first day of school, at six years old, held more promise. There in the classroom on a shelf close to the ceiling, was a statue of a boy dressed like a King in a red robe with a gold crown on his head. In school, I learned that this was Jesus and he had grown up and had performed miracles, had been nailed to a cross, and that he had had risen from the dead. He claimed to be the Son of God. My thoughts raced as I wondered if it had been Jesus that had spoken to me. I earned a prize that year of a statue of Mary, Joseph and Jesus standing together. It was my new prize possession, and I spent a lot of time looking at that statue, mainly at Jesus, wondering about his life.

A Wrong Turn

My search to connect with God had been unceasing. By the time I was eighteen, I determined the church did not have the answer and that Jesus could not have been the voice I had heard at age five. I believed there was a God. I had heard what I had determined to be His voice. I began to focus on books on spirituality.

One day two visitors stopped at the farm to talk about God. I was very interested in hearing all they had to say. They gave me a tract and I read it. The tract stated that Jesus was the Savior of the world. But the information I had read in spiritual books had closed my mind to Jesus. I threw the tract in the trash. I now believed the entire material world was a result of man's 'thoughts', and then man's creation of objects. In my reasoning, if that were true, the trees, dirt, air, sun, moon, stars, all must be a manifestation of God's thoughts. I concluded that to connect with God I just needed to control my thoughts.

I continued to read as much as I could on spirituality and the occult. My life had moved forward. I met the man of my dreams and we got married and purchased a home, and my search continued.

Access to a New Spiritual Dimension

One of the books I had purchased was called, "Three Magic Words". I had been anxious to know what those three magic words were, so I had flipped to the last chapter, and read, "*You* are God." I was amazed by these words. I pondered what this meant. The thought was profound. Suddenly an invisible force jumped on top of me and attacked me. I could see no one but I was being crushed by a spiritual entity. I felt electrical charges going through my body like a knife. I cried out, "Who are you?" A male voice responded, "You opened the door!" The spiritual entity had continued to squash and send sharp electrical charges throughout my body. Instinctively I cried out, "God, please, help me!" Suddenly the thought came into my mind, 'Cling to the cross that Jesus died on.' I closed my eyes and envisioned myself wrapping my arms around that cross. Suddenly the spiritual entity was gone. I sat up and thanked God for intervening and for saving me. I prayed, "Please God; help me to know what to do! Please don't let that happen again!"

I had been successful in getting through into another dimension. But the experience was not what I expected. It was all wrong! This voice was "another voice" not God's voice that had brought me peace and confidence. This voice and the presence of the spiritual entity had produced an awareness of a power larger than anything I had ever experienced; something evil that I could not control.

Answered Prayer

A few days after this attack, I had stopped at a hardware store and had been approached by a new pastor who had come to Vermont to start a Bible believing church in Colchester. Donald Carruth had approached me in the store and asked, "Have you ever read the Bible?" I had replied, "I have not." He continued, "If you died today, are you sure you would go to heaven?" "Of course," had been my reply. He persisted, "When were you married?" I told him the date of my marriage. He replied, "That is the kind of commitment to Christ you should have, a specific time and date that you remember when you committed your life to Christ." He then invited me to attend a Bible study and handed me a leaflet with the time and location. I determined I would go to this Bible study. I purchased a Bible the next day.

In spite of my intense search for God, it had never occurred to me to read the Bible. Now, I wanted to know everything I could about the Bible. To my amazement, the Bible contained accounts of encounters with angels and demonic forces, and most important of all, it contained accounts of not only God's existence, but of His voice from heaven being heard by people on earth. My search for God had been with all my heart, and I had found a book that contained amazing information and answers to my questions.

And you shall seek me, and find me, when you shall search for me with all your heart. Jeremiah 29:13

Chapter 5

Faith = Abundant Life

I had continued to read my new King James Version of the Bible in the New Testament with the accounts of Matthew, Mark, Luke and John. I was surprised that I understood a lot of what I was reading. The miracles of Jesus, the way he lived his life were amazing to me. The words Jesus had spoken were printed in red and they were powerful to me. As I read, I felt the same authority of the voice that had spoken to me when I was five years old.

I read the book of Acts, the letters of Paul, Peter, and John, and the book of Revelation. When I got to this verse in the book of Revelation I stopped. "Behold, I stand at the door and knock, if any man hear my voice, and open the door, I will come in to him and will sup with him and he with me. (Rev. 3:20)

Suddenly I had felt the presence of Jesus standing right beside me. I spoke out loud, "Jesus, I don't know how to get you to come in, but I am opening the door." I waited, but Jesus did not come in. It had taken time for me to understand that for Jesus to come into my heart and life, I needed to make room for him by asking Him for His forgiveness and by accepting His free gift of salvation.

That next Sunday when I attended the Bible study, I found the message very irritating. Amazingly, I had determined I was through with this; when I left that day I would not return. But when I went to leave, a gentleman standing next to the exit moved and stood in front of me. I had tried to go past him, but he had blocked me and said, "I am worried about you, I am afraid when you leave today, you will never return." I was stunned by his verbalization of my thoughts. I replied, "That's not true!" But it was true.

An "I Got It" Moment

As I had continued to walk out, I heard a voice say, "Do you *really* want to go? If you leave now, you are on your own." Immediately I turned around and went back inside. I walked over to Joyce Carruth, the Pastor's wife, and said, "I need to know what to do to be right with God." She took me aside and showed me scriptures in Romans of God's promises that whosoever shall call upon the name of the Lord shall be saved, and she asked me questions regarding what I believed.

As we had talked that day, I understood that salvation was possibly through Jesus's death and resurrection from the cross. I understood that eternal life was free for all and could not be earned by doing good works. We had kneeled together and I repeated a prayer after her, "Lord I believe you died, and I believe you rose again, please forgive me for my sins, please save my soul, and help me to live my life to please Thee." After I had verbalized that prayer, I felt peace flood my body. The peace I felt was beyond explanation and from that moment forward, I knew I was not alone.

The experience had been similar to the energy of electricity inside a light bulb. My life had been like a lamp plugged into a wall. I had equipped myself with the knowledge of the Bible, I knew all about the work of Jesus. I had everything available to be connected to God, just like a lamp that sits on a shelf. But it was only when I actually verbalized and acknowledged my need for Jesus and asked Him to forgive me and save my soul, that a 'spiritual light switch' within me got pushed on. That prayer had opened a pathway for the energy and power of God's Holy Spirit to enter into me, just like electricity enters into a light bulb when the switch is turned on.

And it shall come to pass, that whosoever shall call on the name of the Lord shall be saved. Acts 2:21

Chapter 6

Needs Equal Opportunities

As I had continued to read my Bible, one day I had come to an awesome realization. I closed my Bible and held it up in the air and impulsively said out loud to God, "If all of this is really true, then everything around me, the furniture, the houses, everything in this world, is worthless!" Then without hesitating, I dropped to my knees and said, "Behold the handmaid of the Lord, be it done unto me according to thy word: Send me!"

My life had continued, but it was anything but normal. Things happened that could only be described as divine intervention. I determined that if Jesus got up early to pray, I needed to get up early to pray. Because Jesus kneeled when he prayed, I kneeled when I prayed as well.

One morning while I was on my knees praying for my family I heard God speak clearly, "Your brother is going to kill your mother." Immediately I begged the Lord to intervene.

"Please Lord, you can do all things, please don't let this happen. Send your angels to stop my brother and to protect my mother! Lord, you must intervene, please help! Please don't let this happen!" Over and over I prayed that prayer. Finally I heard the Lord's voice again, "Your mother is going to be okay."

I thanked the Lord for hearing and answering my prayer. I was relieved, but anxious to go to see my mother. I had headed to the farm to visit her. When I entered the kitchen she was standing in front of the kitchen sink in front of a mirror with her back to me. As I looked at her, I could see her face in the mirror, it was very swollen, and her eyes could barely open. I shrieked, "What did my brother do to you?!" Instantly, my Mom turned quickly around and looked at me and exclaimed, "How did you know it was your brother!?" I replied, "The Lord told me when I was praying this morning that he was going to hurt you, and I prayed very hard that the Lord would intervene to protect you." My mother was amazed. We hugged. I helped to fix breakfast and we talked.

My mother told me he had been angry in the barn and had taken a heavy metal connector from a milking machine and had thrown it at her. My mother had seen it coming and had moved, but it had hit her on the side of the temple of her head. My brother had no idea his burst of anger could have killed our Mother that day. Mom held no anger towards him. She asked me not to tell anyone and I assured her I would not.

I did not speak of the event to anyone until after my mother died in 1997. After she had died, I mentioned the incident to my brother. He acknowledged it had happened and felt dreadful about having hurt our Mother and confirmed that he had no idea the metal part would hit her.

That experience of having the Lord speak to me while I was praying and then intervening in answer to my prayer had made me more determined to pray. When I would meet people, and sense a need, I would add them to my prayer list. Before long, I had so many people on my prayer list that I had to categorize them. Because my time to pray was limited, I began to pray a section a day so that I could pray specifically for each person each month.

Years went by. One day as I went through one section of my prayer list, I began to question the purpose of the prayer routine that I had established. "Lord, I think I am overdoing it. I don't think I need to be praying for every person like this."

As I went down the list I pointed to a name on the list, "Look, here is a woman, H. G.! What about her? I met her in an elevator in Burlington. I remember she told me she had just lost her husband. I haven't seen her in years – she could be dead!" I had closed my prayer book, and got up and began my day. But my mind would not stop thinking about it. I made too much of everything. I was such a 'nut'.

My divine experiences that had supported me emotionally and that had helped me justify my actions were useless to me now. I was convinced I was carrying things too far, reading too much into everything. What did I know about anything?!

That afternoon I had needed sewing supplies, so I

traveled to the Ben Franklin Store in Burlington, Vermont. I found the supplies I needed and approached the checkout register. I was behind a woman wearing a beautiful shawl with needlework on it. The shawl was so beautiful I had to comment to her about it.

"What an incredible shawl you have," I said. She turned around to look at me and began to tell me about the shawl. As I heard her voice, I felt the hair on my back stand up. I recognized the voice of H. G., the very woman I had pointed out to the Lord in my prayers that morning. Could this *really* be her?

When she finished speaking, I replied, "I think I know you. I believe we met in an elevator several years ago, you had just lost your husband, and I gave you a poem and a Bible reading. Are you H. G.?" I waited for her response. She got very quiet, and looked closely at me. She then replied, "Yes, I remember you – that was a very long time ago!" I replied, "Yes it was." "How did you know it was me?" she asked. "I've been praying for you," I replied, "and it's good to know you are doing fine." That was all I had said to her, I did not tell her about my conversation with God, or about my prayer list, or how I had challenged God that morning, asking him, "What about H. G.?" I was amazed by it all.

There were so many variables. The name of H. G. on my prayer list that I had randomly picked, the traffic lights, the time I left my home, the time she left her home, the time of my arrival, the time of her arrival, the time to find what I needed, the time for her to find what she needed, and our both ending up in line at the checkout. This was a divine encounter that contained an answer to my question. In fact, God did want us to pray for people individually.

The Black Skirt

The experience with H. G. had helped my faith to grow. One day I determined I needed a new black skirt. My black skirt had started to show wear. I looked through a Penney's catalog and was amazed at the cost for a black skirt. In a dramatic moment, I held up the catalog and said affirmatively out loud, "Lord, if you want me to have a black skirt, give me a black skirt, I am not purchasing one!" I then threw the catalog into the trash bin. Inside I laughed at the possibility of the Lord actually giving me a black skirt. Again I spoke out loud, "Lord, I am so sorry! . I am sure that I can survive without a new black skirt!"

That following Sunday as I went to exit church, Lynne, a church member called out to me, "Wait a minute, I have something for you." In her hand was a grocery bag. "I don't know if you can even use these, but I thought you might be able to," she said. As I looked inside the bag, I could hardly believe my eyes. In that bag was not one, but two black skirts. Of course they both fit perfectly. I had not told anyone about my desire to have a new black skirt. The only one I had spoken to was the Lord the day I had thrown the Penney's catalog in the trash.

I had been amazed the Lord had given me those two black skirts. I praised the Lord and thanked him for providing the skirts, in such an unexpected way.

Now unto him that is able to do exceeding abundantly

above all that we ask or think, according to the power that worketh in us, unto him be glory in the church by Christ Jesus throughout all ages, world without end. Amen. (Ephesians 3:20)

But thou, when thou prayest, enter into thy closet, and when thou hast shut thy door, pray to thy Father which is in secret; and thy Father which seeth in secret shall reward thee openly.

Matthew 6:6

Chapter 7

Before the Throne

God is a Spirit and those that worship Him, must worship Him in

Spirit and in Truth.

John 4:24

I had continued to bring my needs before the Lord and He had continued to provide for my needs and prayers in unexpected ways. The accounting clearly showed life was not about the acquisition of material things. One of my most amazing experiences suddenly flashed back.

An Out of Body Experience

It happened in the middle of the night, and my spirit had been pulled out of my body and suddenly I was on my knees before the Throne of God. Jesus was seated on the throne and there were many people surrounding him.

I was shown my life, like a movie – all the things that

would happen -- including my funeral. I said, "Lord, I don't know *that* many people, how can *that* many people be present?" Jesus did not answer me. He told me instead, "You need to return now. You will remember being before the Throne but you will not remember the sequence of the events of your life or the things you have seen. You will only remember that you were here in heaven before me, and that your life will make no sense."

Suddenly I was back in my body, and in my bed. Instantly, I heard a man's voice next to the bed speak to me. It was an evil spiritual entity.

He clapped his hands loudly three times, and as he clapped, he said, "Let's go! Let's go! Let's go!" As he said those words, he grabbed my physical body and pulled me completely out of bed and onto the floor. My face was pushed into the carpet. The evil spiritual entity attacked me with so much pressure I could hardly breathe and electrical charges were delivered in repeated waves into my back. I prayed, "Lord help me, cover me with your blood! Please help me, please make him go away!"

Again and again the evil spiritual entity hit me as I prayed that prayer over and over. I again envisioned myself clinging to the cross that Jesus died on. It seemed like a very long time before the evil spiritual entity left, but finally he went away and I was free. I got up off the floor and got back into bed. I was shaken but I said out loud, "Thank you Jesus for helping me, thank you so much!"

As I lay on the bed, I thought about everything that had just happened. I pondered all of it for a very long time. Finally I said, "Lord, I don't know what any of this means, but I trust you. You obviously have a plan for me. That is all I need to know. Please protect me from the powers of darkness and help me to do what you would have me to do – *whatever* that is." Amazingly, I had been able to go back to sleep.

After that experience, I began to live each day as though it *might* indeed be my last. I appreciated everything so much more. I was very grateful for having had the privilege of being in heaven and of getting to see and talk to Jesus face-to-face.

And truly what He had told to me had come true: --my life did

not make much sense.

Chapter 8

Instant Death - Be Ready

The reality of the value of time and how it was used had also been clear during the accounting. Things done for the right reason not only mattered, but souls that had been obedient to do even the smallest of things, were so glad they had.

Years passed in my life after I had been before the throne. It felt like I would live forever. And I began to think my experience of being in heaven "Before the Throne" was not what I had thought at all. I concluded that the Lord had allowed me to be in heaven to make sure I would obey Him every day. And even though I had seen my own funeral from heaven, I thought, "I am not going to die anytime soon!"

I continued to live my life and do my work. My mother was put in a nursing home in Morrisville. Because I lived close to Morrisville, I visited her more often. My mom suffered with memory loss. She was not diagnosed officially with Alzheimer's. Our family was told that in order to confirm she had the disease, an autopsy of her brain would be necessary after she died. But my mom had all of the symptoms of Alzheimer's. She did not know any of us anymore, and she had reverted to her native French language. Because I did not understand French, communicating with her had become a challenge. I had come to dread visiting her because it was so heartbreaking to see her and not be recognized.

I remembered the day I received a call from the nursing home asking me to attend a special event in Morrisville. I had agreed to go, but I was not thrilled about going alone. I called family members asking if they could go with me, but all were unable to go that night. When I had gotten home, I had asked my husband to go, but he declined. I had promised to go, so I headed out alone in my car.

Once past Cambridge, Vermont the road to Morrisville has rolling hills, up and down hills -- hills, hills, and more hills. I remembered pressing on the gas, I wanted to get there quicker. I would go and do what needed to be done, so I could go home!

My car picked up speed, as I went up and down over the hills. Suddenly I heard God's voice say, "Slow down!" Startled, I immediately took my foot off the gas and immediately reached down to turn on my tape player. This took only a few seconds. When I lifted my eyes back onto the road, my car was cresting the top of a hill and right in front of me was a car in my lane passing two vehicles! I thought, "This is it!"

I had no time to even put my foot on the brake or to think any thoughts about my life. I looked directly into the eyes of a young male driver who was about 16 or17 years old. He was terrified -- I was terrified. His car was traveling at least 90-100 miles an hour.

I had watched as he turned his steering wheel fast with his hands to the right. His car swerved immediately to the right and went sideways off the road into the ditch. He had missed hitting the front of my car by less than an inch and he had missed hitting the car that he was passing by also less than an inch.

Just as quickly, I watched as he turned his steering wheel quickly to the left. His speed pulled his vehicle out of the ditch and back onto the road. I then had locked eyes with the driver of the car that he was passing. We looked at each other in total disbelief. Now the driver in the second car locked eyes with me in total disbelief. My car continued over the crest of the hill and down the other side. I had immediately pulled over and stopped by the side of the road. My knees and hands were shaking uncontrollably; my heart pounded. Miraculously I was fine. Our vehicles had not even touched each other.

I had sat in my car on the side of the road for a long time calming myself down. I thought of the enormous speed of the teenage driver and how that speed had worked in our favor. How his quick reaction to turn the wheel quickly right and then quickly left had prevented us from colliding at the top of that hill.

But I knew something the teenager and both of the other drivers did not know. God had told me to "slow down' and I had taken my foot off the gas. My car had slowed down providing us with those few extra seconds that had given the teenager time to turn the wheel and spare us from colliding at the top of the hill.

I was convinced that without those few extra seconds, that driver would not have had time to turn the wheel. We would have just 'hit.' It is also quite possible that because of his speed, any collision could have caused our two vehicles to spin around into the paths of the other two vehicles. And with his incredible speed, there would have been injuries and possibly fatalities.

I also believed it was the presence of the Lord inside of that teenager that actually turned the wheel of that car that saved all of us. It all happened so fast! It seemed surreal. Surely someone also was praying for us! I recalled the many times that someone's name suddenly entered my mind during my day, and I had quickly offered up a prayer on their behalf.

I thanked the Lord for sparing me, and for reminding me how quickly he could take me at any time. And I remembered God's message to me in heaven regarding my own funeral when I was "Before the Throne". I continued onto the nursing home. I visited my Mom that night and went home.

But God's voice telling me to `slow down' and the car passing on that hill had made me aware that each day is a gift and that all tasks are privileges, even when they are an obligation.

The accounting was clear, the Lord is aware of our circumstances, wherever we are and he is able to help us through each day. He is able to do abundantly above and beyond all that we ask or think, and intervenes on our behalf, even before we are aware that we need his help.

Be strong and of a good courage; be not afraid, neither be dismayed: for the LORD your God is with you wherever you go.

Joshua 1:9

Chapter 9

Much Given/Much Required: SIGNS

And there shall be signs . . . in the moon. Luke 21:25

During the accounting, some individuals had been more accountable than others. They had received more and therefore had more to give an account for. Those that had done wrong, but had not been aware that what they were doing was wrong, received mercy, and those that knew they were doing wrong, and did it anyway, lost rewards.

I remembered that my own accountability was very high. Because I was aware that I could be taken at any time, I had a desire to work hard to fill my days with service to the Lord. But beyond that, there was one night that forever had changed my life and my awareness of the times in which I lived.

The Appearance of Jesus

I had been with my husband and we were getting ready

to go to bed. I remembered hearing the excitement in his voice as he exclaimed to me, "There's a full moon tonight!"

I had listened without enthusiasm, and humored him with my reply, "Really!" We were descending down two sets of stairs to the basement, when he grabbed my waist as we went down and exclaimed again, excitedly, "Yes, yes, a full moon!" His brother and his wife were visiting from Massachusetts. We had readied our upstairs bedroom for them for the night and we were retiring to a sofa bed in our unfinished basement. I thought, "How odd for him to be so excited about a full moon!" He usually wasn't very expressive or excited about anything. A full moon meant little to nothing to me. My thoughts were on how we both would sleep in that sofa bed!

We had entered the unfinished basement and we worked together to pull out the sofa bed. I walked over to side of the bed next to the window. I had looked out the window to see if I could see a full moon, but there was nothing to see. We settled down and fell asleep.

At about 1:15 am, I had awakened to a stream of light

from a huge full moon hitting my face. The moon had been perfectly centered in the window and was filling the basement with light. I checked to see if my husband was awake. No, he was not. I thought, should I wake him? He was sound asleep beside me. No, I would not wake him. We both had to work the next day and we both needed our sleep. As I looked at the moon, I began to pray and talk to Jesus. As I talked and prayed, suddenly the face of Jesus appeared in the moon. I remembered him from seeing him in heaven. His hair was black and curly, short, and shiny. His skin was light and fair; and he had no beard. His eyes were a crystal blue and they shined very brightly. Instantaneously I waved to him with my hand and said, "Hi Jesus!" As I had continued to wave excitedly, my mind thought, 'this is crazy; you can't be seeing Jesus, you just can't!' But there was Jesus's face in the moon, as big as the moon itself!

"Okay, Jesus," I said, "I see you, but my mind doesn't believe that this is happening! I am going to close my eyes and then open them again. If you are really there, when I open my eyes again you should *still* be there." I had then closed my eyes. When I opened my eyes again, Jesus's face was gone. The full moon was still there, just as bright as ever, but Jesus was gone. I had felt a bit sad, but also a bit relieved.

As I continued to look at the moon, I continued to talk to Jesus. I told Him again how much I loved Him, and that I wanted to serve Him. Then suddenly just as before, he appeared again! This time He smiled at me, a half smile – with part of his lip curling up on the right while the other half of his mouth stayed straight. He did not speak to me, or say a word, but He kept the smile on his face. His face remained in the moon for about a minute and then He disappeared again. Then my heart began to beat very fast.

I had looked over at my husband. Had he seen him too? No, he was fast asleep. Should I wake him and tell him? If I did, what would he say? Surely he would say it was a dream, go back to sleep. But I could not sleep, it was not a dream. I was wide awake. I had to get up. I had to pray. I had to know, "What did this mean?" I wanted confirmation. As I got up, my mind told me, 'What just happened could not have possibly happened!' But it HAD happened and not once; but twice, and my husband had been so excited about the moon before we even had gone to bed – that in itself was so odd!

Bible Confirmation

I had NOT sought this out, and never would have expected anything like this to ever happen. Why, why, WHY?? I had proceeded upstairs to the kitchen area. As my heart pounded, I become hot and sweaty. I grabbed my Bible and sat down on the floor in the kitchen. I told the Lord, "If this is real, confirm this to me from your word."

I randomly opened my Bible – the book opened to pages of John 13 and 14 in the New Testament. As I read scriptures on both sides of these two pages, I came to this verse:

He that hath my commandments and keepeth them, he it is that loveth me, and he that loveth me shall be loved of my Father, and I will love him and will manifest myself to him.

(John 14:21).

"Manifest" means 'show' or 'reveal.' I thanked the Lord for appearing to me the first time, the second time, and for his assurance from the Bible that I had indeed seen Him. I dated the verse in my Bible 6-28-80, and went back downstairs to the basement to bed.

In the morning, my husband and I got ready for work, and we rode together so I could drop him off at work. As he drove, he asked, "What's going on?" I was very quiet. "Are you okay?" he asked. I decided I *would* tell him what happened. "I saw Jesus in the moon last night, just his head, and he smiled at me." There was silence on his end. He did not answer or say a word. I affirmed and said, "I know it sounds crazy, but I saw Jesus in the moon!" My husband had looked at me but said nothing. As we arrived at his work and he got out of the car, he said, "We can talk about this later." But we never did talk about it that day, or ever. I had decided from that experience, I would not tell anyone else about it. But for days, weeks, and months after, I walked and felt like I was in a fog.

Eternal Moments

That had been over thirty-two years ago. I had drawn Jesus's face in my Bible in several places. I was looking forward to seeing Him again when I entered into His kingdom. Jesus had never appeared to me again in that way. It was my belief that this was a 'sign' that we were indeed in the last days before His return to the earth in the air. The sight of a full moon from thereafter would forever fill me with wonder and joy.

I also believed others had also seen Jesus's face in the moon, as I did not believe I could be the only one. The Bible indeed says there will be signs in the last days in the sun and in the moon and in the stars. It was my prayer that the Lord would open our hearts and minds to the truth of His word. That He would unstop our ears, and open our eyes, and deliver us from the love of this world, the lust of this flesh and the pride of this life, and that He would not let not the powers of the enemy be greater than His power to intervene on our behalf, to redeem, restore, recover, and deliver us from evil.

I prayed that His will would be done on earth as it is in heaven and that His house would be full of the praise that is due His holy name. I prayed that He would deliver us from the sins of greed, corruption, pride and lack of love for one another and disobedience to His word.

And as the cup of iniquity on earth continues to fill, it is His promise that 'iniquity will have an end' that provides comfort, and encouragement for us to not be unbelievers, but rather to believe that He is able to accomplish His will on earth.

Chapter 10

More than the Body – Walking Tin Man

For in him we live, and move, and have our being." Acts 17:28

The accounting revealed something very obvious – physical bodies were just 'turtle shells' for the soul. Vessels designed as containers and life was more than eating, drinking and making merry. There was a much higher purpose to it all. We were more than just the body.

Bodily Divine Control

My memory recalled an experience where God had taken control of my body, while I was still in it.

Each year there had been missionary alliance retreats, and one year I was invited to attend. I traveled with a church group to this retreat. At the end of the week, there had been a special missionary speaker. As the missionary finished her talk and the congregation of people began to sing, I heard the Lord tell me "Go forward." I had replied," I don't think so." Again, clearly, "Go." And again, I told the Lord, "I don't want to go." Again I was told, "Go."

The song finished and people had gone forward, but not me; I sat down, I said, "Just let me sit here until this is over." Another song started. Suddenly I had felt an incredible ball of energy stir inside me in the core of my abdomen. The energy rushed and swirled and grew larger and larger. The energy was like a tornado of energy and suddenly it grew so large that without warning, it lifted me up onto me feet and moved me right out of the pew into the isle and up to the sanctuary altar. My feet went up and down, mechanically. I was like a walking tin man. I was going forward after all! My hands grasped the song book I had been holding. I was marched right up onto the altar, where the missionary was seated in a chair.

As I approached her, she looked quizzically at me. The energy then dropped me to my knees in front of her and the book in my hand fell into her lap. The force of energy that had magically propelled me forward, had now switched out of me. I looked down at the song book, the titles of the songs were,

"Crown Him with Many Crowns" and "The King is Coming." I then looked at the missionary and said, "Surely Jesus is coming, look at the titles of the songs!" As I looked at the song book now on her lap, I noticed the pattern on her skirt had hundreds of golden crowns all over it. I exclaimed, "Wow, look at all the crowns on your skirt!" She replied, "Never mind about that, the King *is* coming. Yes, I know."

Experiential Understanding

That experience had forever changed me. My understanding expanded in an experiential way. I knew the Lord is 'Spirit' and His 'Holy Spirit' is everywhere. He is able to do abundantly above and beyond all things. He is even able to move a body when we are unwilling to go, to accomplish whatever He requires. Truly, "In Him we **do** live and move and have our being."

I understood how it is possible for a human being to lift a car to save someone. The wonder for me was how I could possibly 'think' I could do anything all by myself. Truly the body is just a "glove" for our soul. My awareness of my body being just a vessel to learn and experience life was solidified by this experience.

The closest I had come to feeling totally controlled by God since that happened, was through fasting and prayer which reconnected me to this awareness. It was a comfort to know this, because it is reassurance that we are never alone wherever we happen to be in whatever circumstances. And "He" is ours to the degree that we allow him to be. It is through clean minds and hearts that we give him room to occupy and guide our thoughts. His Word, the Bible, contains His thoughts and the more it is read, understood, and applied; the greater that we sense His peace, joy and love, and the greater our awareness of His presence becomes.

Faith comes by hearing the Word of God. When we focus on serving God and each other --that is when God can use our circumstances to exercise and grow our faith.

Chapter 11

Redeem the Time – Obedience

Another amazing reality during the soul's accounting was the fact that some souls had gained a greater knowledge of the reality of God during their lifetimes than others. The reason was clear. Some had actually followed Jesus Christ's example and had laid down their life and had used their time differently and had been available to God for His use.

My own life accounting would include an amazing experience of that kind of service.

I remembered clearly how that day had started. I had got up and said, "Lord, what would you have me do today?" My day was wide open, without commitments. I had finished reading my Bible and dressed, thanking the Lord for my beautiful home, and for providing for me. I had said, "Truly the desire of my heart is to please you Lord, so just let me know what I should do with my time."

Suddenly a thought flashed through my mind,

'blackberries.' I said, "Well, Lord, I can go and search for some blackberries." We had moved to Jericho. Being new to the area, I thought, there must be blackberries around here somewhere. I wondered if it was too early for them, but I would go and look. Pail in hand, off I went, up the hill and into the field that went along a wooded area. I walked to a fence line and stopped. I could see nothing. "Surely there must be some blackberries here, Lord." I had said, as I had gotten down on my knees to look under a thorn bush.

To my amazement, under the thorn bush, I could see a few huge blackberries. These blackberries would be hard to get. I slid myself on my back under the fence and under the branches of the thorn bush. Once under the bush, I could see tons of blackberries; huge big ones, perfectly ripe and ready for picking. As I crawled on my back and carefully picked, my bucket filled. Each blackberry seemed to be longer and fatter as I worked to the center of the trunk of the bush. The deeper in they were, the BIGGER they were! These were the largest blackberries I had ever seen, and they were sweet and juicy as well.

It was a lot of work to get in, and then to get myself back out under the fence. My arms were scratched, but I was happy as I started walking home. I then asked, "Lord, whatever shall I do with all of these blackberries? There are just so many of them!"

As I prayed and thought about the people I knew, I thought about my friend Sue White. I had not called her in quite a while. We were usually very busy; both of us always seemed to have a lot to do. Once home, I picked up the phone and dialed. I wondered if she would even be home. I said to the Lord, "She might not be home. She might not even like blackberries." The phone rang and to my amazement she answered, and she had time to talk.

We chatted and got caught up on our lives. I then said, "Sue, I have a question for you and you can say "no" you might not even like or want them, but I have some blackberries, would you like some?" The phone was silent.

I added, "You don't need to take them Sue, I know not everyone likes them, but they are really sweet and the biggest blackberries I have ever seen." She replied, "That's not it." I asked, "Well, what is it?" Again there was silence on the phone.

Finally she said, "You are not going to believe this Dawn, yesterday I told the Lord I really wanted some blackberries, but I did not have the time to go pick them -- if He wanted me to have blackberries, he would have to bring them to me. Now, you call this morning and ask me if I want blackberries!" I replied, "Oh, my goodness! Sue, I asked the Lord what he would have me to do today, and I thought of blackberries, I haven't been blackberry picking in years." There was again dead silence on the phone.

Neither of us spoke as we reflected on the magnitude of what was happening. This was answered prayer, unity of thought and oneness created for each of us -- a miracle neither of us would ever forget.

I delivered those blackberries to her that day, and time

marched on, but the blackberries were a reminder of the power of the Lord to meet our needs in unusual ways when we least expect it.

Each of us walks different paths and we are all different. What a wonder it is that through reading God's word and reflecting on how we might serve him, He opens up the windows of heaven. It is through our 'obedience' that His Holy Spirit can lead us to answers to our prayers.

It is when we obey God in the one "thing" that the next thing opens up. It is obedience that opens heaven. Sometimes God's silences are His answer. The blessings come when we cannot go any further without them. I also had learned that silence was also a place to trust Him.

Lord, help us to have faith and know that you do hear our prayers! Help us to have you as our portion: Christ as Redeemer, Spirit, Guide, Sanctifier, and Comforter. Help us to seek 'divine currency' thru obedience to your word, because it is then that we shall 'ask what we will and it shall be done unto us.'

Lord, help us to remember that truth and charity are loveliest when they walk hand in hand. For the fashion of this "world" is passing away.

Lord, grant us grace to live above these "things." Let us not set our hearts upon them, or care whether we have them or have them not, help us rather to exercise all our energy in pleasing Thee and in gaining those things that Thou dost esteem: the true riches of grace.

Chapter 12

God is Spirit - The Light

Life on earth was more than just the 'body", the soul within needed nourishment. Like fish need water to survive, the soul within needs renewal through abiding in the Word of God to come alive. For everything material is temporary and only the invisible is eternal. The Bible although written long ago, contains truths as well as the presence of the Holy Spirit. And the reality of the presence of the Holy Spirit would also be part of my accounting.

My life was filled with activities and commitments and I was usually tired and I welcomed night and the opportunity to go to bed. On this night I had been happy, too, that my husband was working a midnight shift, because it gave me the entire bed to myself. I had gone to bed early that night. I was sleeping fine until I felt a 'push' that awoke me.

When I opened my eyes to see who had pushed me, I was amazed by a bright light that was coming into the bedroom. Through that light I looked around the room. There was no one in the bedroom only that light that was very bright but very narrow. It looked like a laser beam. It was coming into the room through the wall over the top of the bed.

I had been sleeping on my stomach with my head lying to the right side. I picked up my head to see where the light was coming into the room. I worked to answer questions in my mind. What was happening here? Why was a light coming through the wall, and where was it coming from?

I continued to lift my head to look towards its source to see exactly where it was entering the room. As I did so, my head was suddenly pushed down into my pillow and locked firmly in place. Now, I could not move my head at all.

The light became centered on the top of my head and began to penetrate into my skull. This laser beam light was very hot and it was boring what felt like a hole inside my brain. I could do nothing to stop it. My skull heated up and then I heard a loud 'pop' inside my head. The light then released my head and I was free to move again.

Warm energy flooded through my body. The energy went down through my neck, into my chest, arms, and legs and into my toes. This warm hot energy passed through me like a wave, back and forth, inside my body. Back and forth, from the tip of my head to my toes, back and forth, back and forth, the wave traveled. The warmth felt incredibly wonderful and brought with it an indescribable peace.

When the waves of warm energy subsided, I turned myself over. I felt the top of my head which was still hot to my touch. There was no hole in my head. The light had left as quickly as it had arrived. I got up and turned on my bedroom light to examine the wall where the light had come in.

There was no window in that wall and the light had not created any hole in the wall. Neither was there any scorching mark on the wall where the light had come through. I lay back down in my bed and thought about what had just happened. Other than the "pop" inside my head, I felt physically no different.

I wondered, was this the anointing of the Holy Spirit

upon me? The next day my level of peace continued beyond anything I had known. And as time passed, I continued to experience new levels of understanding. Divine interactions continued to occur that defied explanation. When I read the Bible, I felt as though what was described had *just* happened. My interactions with people intensified and my prayers became more encompassing.

I had told the Lord, "The need in the world for awareness of salvation is so great; so much work needs to be done, and so few seem willing to do it. I am not much, but I am here." This was an answered prayer. And there appeared unto them cloven tongues like as of fire, and it sat upon each of them. (Acts 2:3)

This was what the apostles experienced. This was an anointing of the Holy Spirit, the flaming tongue of fire, similar to those that came down upon their heads of the apostles after Christ had risen from the dead.

Chapter 13

Grace Transforms - Forgiveness

Then came Peter to him, and said, Lord, how oft shall my brother sin against me, and I forgive him? Till seven times? Jesus saith unto him, I say not unto thee, until seven times: but, until seventy times seven. Matthew 18:22

Wrongs were disclosed during the accounting, some of which were forgiven, some were not. My own life included one large opportunity to forgive and one large opportunity to be forgiven. The opportunity to forgive occurred when I was eleven years old: my forgiveness for that incident would not happen until I was over fifty years old.

Being a babysitter was a big part of my life and neighbors enjoyed our family's large selection of girls. When I was eleven years old, I began babysitting for our new neighbors who had moved in next door. They had two small children. The family stayed next door for just one summer, but that summer would have a dramatic impact on my life.

Forty Years Later

In 1989, my closest friend Patti Pratt died and I was totally distraught. I went for death counseling. When I arrived I was taken into a small room that had one window and one door. I was seeing a male counselor who began to talk with me about death and dying. I was extremely uncomfortable and could not concentrate on anything he said.

My eyes darted back and forth between the door and the window, and fear arose within me. All I could focus on was the male counselor's nose that was larger than normal. The session ended and I left. Once I had returned home, I went and sat on my couch. I told the Lord, "I am not leaving this couch, until I know why I felt so afraid in that room."

An hour passed. I thought 'this is ridiculous' and I got up and started to walk away, but before I could even get into the next room, I stopped, myself and returned to the couch and sat down. "Lord, I am not leaving this couch until I understand this, even if it takes the rest of the day and night."

There I sat. I picked up a magazine but immediately made myself put it down. I determined I would do nothing, read nothing: I would just sit and wait for an answer. I looked out the window. It was a beautiful day but I was not going outside to enjoy it.

It did not take long after that for a sudden mental flashback to occur. A quick mental image appeared. I saw the face of a man with a large nose, the same size nose that the counselor had, and that man was chasing me around a room that had one door and one window. More flashbacks followed. I had been molested at eleven by the neighbor for whom I had been a babysitter and he had threatened to kill me if I told anyone.

Divine Cleansing

I prayed for help to forgive the man who had molested me. The house where the molestation had occurred would be burned to the ground. The day the house burned, I stood and watched on our farm porch as the house literally disappeared.

Not having to travel past the house produced healing, but more healing would follow. That fall, one of my sisters phoned to tell me she had seen the man who molested me on the local news. He had been arrested for collecting money for work that had not been done. Again, I asked the Lord to help me forgive and to help me to continue to pray for him.

An Unexpected Delivery

One day while I was at work, I was asked to go mail a package at the Burlington Post Office. When I arrived, I looked at the line of people in front of me. Suddenly, I realized that I was behind the very man who had molested me. He was in front of me in line and there were two people between us.

I assessed the situation and determined I would not have to interact with him. He would be out of the post office before me. I finished mailing my package, and turned to leave.

I was shocked when I looked to see the man standing at

the exit door holding the door open for me. As I approached

the door he announced, "A gentlemen always opens the door

for a lady!" I replied, "Well I am a lady, but you are anything

but a gentleman! Do you have any idea who I am? No, you

have no idea who I am, do you?"

Now people began gathering at the entrance. He was

visibly embarrassed by me. I was through the door now, but I

could not stop myself. I turned around and looked at him and

said, "You molested me when I was eleven years old!" His face

got red and he shouted, "I'm sorry!" I replied, "Sorry doesn't

cut it! You ruined my life." Again he said, "I'm sorry, I've been

to counseling for that!" As I walked away, I said, "Being sorry

doesn't change anything, you stole part of my life from me."

I was shaken by this encounter, but proud that I had

spoken the truth. Truly the Lord had orchestrated the chance

meeting to help me to heal. I continued to pray for him.

The Unexpected Cost

A new reality had become painfully obvious. I had

disconnected from my husband and our relationship was strained. One day I had walked into the living room of our home and said, "I have to leave. I cannot stay with you. I feel like I want to yell at you all the time and I don't even know who I am anymore." I left that day and never returned.

Our home was sold and both of us continued with separate lives. For this transgression, I have had to work hard to forgive myself, and have asked for forgiveness from my former husband.

Forgiveness Counts

I would be given one more divine opportunity to forgive the man who molested me.

One Christmas Eve when I turned fifty, I went with friends for brunch to a popular restaurant for a brunch buffet. I followed them to a booth they had selected. As I went to sit down, I looked in amazement at the bar. Sitting on a bar stool seated to the left of our booth that we would sit in, was the man who had molested me. My friends watched as my face turned pale.

As I sat down, they asked, "What's wrong?" I replied, "Well, the man who molested me when I was eleven is seated on that bar stool," as I pointed to the bar stool. They looked over at him and then back at me in disbelief. They asked, "What are you going to do?" I replied, "Nothing, I have forgiven him."

We ordered and our lunch arrived. We visited, but out of the corner of my eye I had a full view of this man as he ate his lunch. A mirror was in front of him at the bar, and I could see his face clearly. As he ate, his eyes stayed fixed at the corner of the restaurant. I looked to see what was drawing his attention. There at a table in that corner of the restaurant was a young girl who was having lunch with her parents.

She wore a summer dress. He could not keep his eyes off of her. When she got up to go to the buffet for food with her family, his head followed her. I watched in disbelief. The man was now close to seventy years old. He had dyed his hair jet black, and wore tight jeans, and had rolled up his shirt sleeves to reveal arm muscles that no longer existed. What I saw was a man imprisoned by the lusts of the flesh.

The family with the young girl finished their meal and he finished his. The family left. He also got up to leave. As he passed our table, he made eye contact with me and said, "Have a good day!" Suddenly I realized I needed to talk to him. When I went to get up, my friends said in disbelief, "Are you going to talk to him?" I replied, "Yes."

I had to walk fast now to catch up to him. I yelled his name and he stopped and looked around. Now he recognized me. The last time we met, I had been in the Post Office and I had yelled at him. He snarled at me, "What do you want?" I said, "You need to know I have forgiven you." He replied, "Is that it?" I said, "No, I have something for you," and I handed him a Bible tract. He said, "What should I do with this?" I replied, "I suggest you read it! There is a prayer on the back. I suggest you say it." He left, and I went back to the table to my friends. They asked, "What did you say?" I replied, "I told him that I forgave him!" That Christmas the Lord gave me one of the best presents I had ever received. The opportunity to actually meet and tell someone that I had really forgiven them for a wrong that had been done to me.

Divine Empowerment

We as believers have something that is the most valuable thing in the whole world. We have the freedom to change and to become different people. We are not locked into the lusts of the flesh, or to the lusts of the eye, or to the pride of life, or to the love of this world. It is through faith in the Lord's work on the cross that our lives become transformed. And it is the act of truly forgiving that sets us free.

Chapter 14

Ask and ye shall receive - Buffy

Most souls had to account for selfish prayers that had been answered, and many discounted answered prayers as just coincidences. I knew better. In the spiritual realm there were no coincidences.

A Selfish Prayer

Although I prayed all the time for God's help, it was rare for me to ask Him for anything material. The understanding between me and Him was that He would meet my needs. My job was to be obedient to His leading, to read and know His Word, to pray without ceasing. and to be there to help wherever I was, in whatever way that I could. Sometimes that was simply taking out the trash, or doing the dishes, or picking up a piece of trash on the ground and putting it where it belonged.

Sometimes it was praying for someone who I thought of

'out of the blue' and calling to see how they were doing. Oftentimes, it was just showing up and doing whatever needed to be done to the best of my ability, even when I didn't feel the greatest. And many times it involved sharing my faith and scriptures with others, encouraging them to read the Bible, and praying for them that the Lord would speak to their hearts and open their minds to the truth that nothing goes unnoticed in the spiritual world.

A New Beginning

After my divorce I had met a man and had fallen in love. He was a Christian and we planned to get married and we purchased a condo together. Soon after we met, his lifelong pet Sebastian died. He had two cats and he had gotten Sebastian as a kitten. He and Sebastian had bonded as 'one' so the loss of his cat was large. The solution I felt was to obtain another furry friend for him, but he was not ready.

As we approached October, he asked me to think about what I would like for Christmas. Instinctively and instantaneously I replied, "I would like a cat! But this cat cannot be just any ordinary cat. What I want is an orange cat that is free, spayed, declawed, and female." His reaction was classic, "Well, I'll start looking today, but that is a lot to be asking for and I am not sure we will find a cat that meets all of your criteria."

The Search

So the search began. Every day he would check the newspaper, the animal shelters and ads in stores. And every once in a while he would tell me he had found a potential cat. But each time, the cat located was missing one or two of the criteria. I would say, "No, that cannot be the cat." He would reply, "You can't expect to find a cat with all of those criteria! It is not going to happen!"

But I had total confidence in the power of God to answer my prayer. I was adamant, "If God wants me to have a cat, that cat must meet all of those criteria. If we cannot find a cat that meets those requirements, then it will be obvious that God does not want me to have a cat."

Time passed, and there was no cat. A few days before Christmas he said, "I hate to tell you this, but you are not going to get a cat for Christmas. There isn't any that meet the standards you have demanded." I said nothing. I was heartbroken. I went upstairs to be alone and to talk to God.

I entered a spare bedroom and got down on my knees and sobbed. I was not prone to cry, ever, and to cry was totally out of character for me. As I was able to form words between my gasps for air between my sobbing, I said, "Lord, it isn't like I need a cat. That is not why I am crying. The reason I am crying is because I never ask you for anything. You ask me to do things all the time, and I always try to do whatever you ask me to do. Here, now, I ask you for a cat. You are God, you can do anything! Giving me a cat that meets the criteria is nothing for you to do, you created cats!

What makes me *so* sad is that after all I have done for you, you are telling me 'no' that I cannot have a cat. But I trust that you have a reason why you will not give me a cat. I am crying because I am sad that I have not pleased you enough for you to answer this prayer." I wiped away my tears, blew my nose, and returned downstairs.

As I entered our living room I announced, "It's okay that I won't be getting a cat for Christmas. Obviously God does not want me to have a cat. Why don't you start looking for a cat and it will be your new cat." "But I have nothing for you for Christmas," he said. I replied, "That is not a problem, I have you."

The Advertisement

Things settled down and the days passed until the morning of Christmas Eve. When I came downstairs he was very excited, "I think I have found your cat!" I was astounded, "Let me see."

There in the newspaper under "FREE" was an advertisement: CAT: "Buffy" female, spayed, declawed, orange, with a phone number. It was not yet 7 am, but I picked up the phone and called the number. I said to the person who answered the phone, "I am calling about your ad for Buffy; I would like to come and get her." The man replied, "Well, Buffy cannot go to just anyone." I said, "No, you don't understand, Buffy is my cat, I have been praying for her for over three months," He replied, "You can come and look at her, but I am not promising that I will give her to you until I meet you." I said, "That's fine, please give me directions." I hung up the phone and said, "Buffy is in Rochester Vermont. Where is Rochester?" We looked on a map. Rochester was three hours away.

We got ready and left immediately. It was a long ride. My friend was not sure we would come back with the cat. I assured him that Buffy was mine and that this was indeed an answered prayer.

We pulled up into the driveway of the address, and we went to the door. The man greeted us. Buffy came to the door and sniffed my pants. The man stood speechless. He said, "Well, she has *never* done that before with anyone, she must be yours! In fact, you can also have her toys, her litter box, her carrier, and her bed as well." Tears welled up in my eyes.

Buffy was the sweetest cat I had ever met. We thanked the man profusely. He had no idea what the last three months had been like for both of us.

Healing Old Wounds

The reason I had determined this cat needed to be orange was to heal a wound from my childhood. When I was about ten years old, my sisters picked names for the cats that lived in the barn and chose them as their cats. There was one male sick orange cat they named "Ringworm" because he was missing fur on different parts of his body. "Ringworm" was designated to be *my* cat.

When they brought "Ringworm" to me, I was disheartened. Not only did he have ringworms but he also had no tail. He had lost it in the blade of the engine that powered the milking machines. Because my first cat had been orange, I felt it fitting that any cat I acquired as an adult should also be orange.

The Long Ride Home

Buffy cried all the way home in the car for our three-hour trip back. Once we got her inside the house she ran upstairs to the very bedroom where I had cried my eyes out and there she hid under the bed for three solid days and nights. Each morning and night I brought food and milk to her and got down on my knees to talk to her under the bed. Finally she came out.

Buffy was my miracle cat. She died in 2009 and I keep a picture of her on my desk at work.

Buffy would not be my only orange cat. One of my sister's had taken kittens that had been found in one of the barns into her home. She fed and nursed them, transforming them from snarling, scratching wild animals, to loving sweet kittens. One of the kittens was male and orange, and she asked me if I would like to have him.

The moment I saw him, I named him, "Wilson" from the movie, "Castaway". Once he was fully weaned 'Wilson' became my second orange cat. As a kitten, I would put Wilson on my shoulder and take him for walks with me. He now weighs about 20 lbs.

But it is the story of Buffy that moves me to tears whenever I recall the circumstances behind how she came into my life. She is like an 'exclamation point' in my mind representing the power of the Lord to not only answer prayers, but to answer them in His time, even though the mathematical probability is statistically impossible.

Making No Sense

One of the most challenging decisions of my life was to walk away from the second wonderful man in my life. I was still unable to communicate my needs and decided to be on my own so I could heal emotionally. One of my sisters invited me to stay with her, and I took her up on her offer.

Now faith is the substance of things hoped for, the evidence of things not seen. Hebrews 11:1

Chapter 15

Everything Counts - God's Hand

During the accounting, everything counted, no small act of kindness had ever been wasted. Each life had had many different paths, and each decision had caused one path to open and others to close.

My accounting would include one specific door closing and another one opening. During my divorce my husband had asked for only one thing, that I not take money from his retirement fund. Although by law I was entitled to half of the funds, I agreed to not ask for that money. After I had agreed, I said to the Lord, "Surely it was a foolish thing for me to agree to not take that money. I then prayed and asked the Lord to return those funds to me tenfold."

A Place to Call Home

Although I had saved some money, I had not saved enough to purchase much of a house. My Dad agreed to provide land that he owned for building a house for both of us.

He had gifted ten acres of land that he owned to one of my sisters who had built a home on the land. Their agreement was for her to deed back seven acres to him when he was ready so he could build a home. When we called her, she agreed immediately to return the seven acres to him, so I could build a home for us. I went to the Town Clerk and filed the paperwork for a subdivision. The paperwork was then mailed to my sister to be signed and returned to the Town, and the search for a building plan began. My Dad suggested that I look at a house that had been built by his friends in Highgate Center. The layout he felt would be perfect for us. I visited the home and my Dad had been correct. The home was just what we would need. It was a small ranch with an upper level and a lower level that could be finished into an apartment.

But things would not go according to plan. I was notified my one of my other sisters that there would be no transfer of property for building on my Dad's land. I was disheartened and confused. I went to talk with my Dad, but he was not willing to even discuss it. My sister who now owned that land had her reasons and he would not challenge her decision.

When I had looked at the home in Highgate Center, the owners had given me an electrical panel that I could use for building our home. I went to return that panel and explained that I would not be building a home after all. I said, "If you ever want to sell your home, please let me know." Amazingly they told me they were thinking of selling their home in about two years. They wanted to sell just the house and one acre. I told them I would be very interested in purchasing the home and to keep me posted.

Going With the Flow

I began looking for extra jobs and worked as much as I could, doing whatever I could. I had two years to raise funds to purchase that home. An opportunity arose for me to purchase a new condo that was being built, and I decided to buy it and sell it once it was completed to gain extra funds.

Just as the condo was completed, I received a call

from my Dad's friends. They were ready to sell within a year but had heard that I had purchased a condo. I explained that I had purchased the condo in order to purchase their home and would sell it immediately.

The condo sold within a month and I gained $7,000 from the transaction. That sale had given me just enough money to qualify to purchase their home for their asking price of $195,000. But when it came time to sign the Purchase and Sales Agreement, the owners had decided they did not want to sell just the house and one acre, but the entire property and they were asking for an additional $40,000 for the extra two acres. The home was reappraised with the extra two acres but it did not appraise for their asking price. I now had one month before our closing to acquire an extra $35,000 to purchase the home.

I prayed and asked the Lord to help me do just that. It occurred to me that if I did purchase the home, I could rent the home as a vacation spot. It was located on a manmade lake, and had a boat and a dock. I approached individuals at work and offered them a week's vacation at my new home during the summer. I explained that if I was unable to come up with the entire amount necessary to purchase the home, I would return their checks immediately. Amazingly there were individuals who wrote checks and signed up for specific weeks.

Even with all my efforts, I was still short $25,000. I prayed and asked the Lord to help me. I contacted TIAA-CREF to see if I could use funds from my retirement account to purchase the home, but they told me I could not. I even called friends to see if I could borrow money, but I could not. I had done everything I could. It would take a miracle for me to be able to come up with the additional funds.

After a long weekend of adjusting to the thought of not being able to purchase the property, I went to work Monday morning. As I turned the key to unlock my office, I said, "Lord, I have done all I can and I just can't make this happen."

The Miracle Phone Call

As I sat down at my work desk my phone rang. The first

call of the day was from a representative of Fidelity. The gentleman on the phone apologized for not calling me back sooner. I replied, "Well, I do not want to talk to you today about anything. I am having a very sad day." He asked, "What is going on?" I replied, "I cannot purchase the home I want because I am short funds to do so." He asked, "Is this the first home you are purchasing?" I replied, "Yes, I have owned a home before with my former husband, but I have never purchased a home all by myself." He replied, "Well, you can borrow 50% of the funds in your account that you have contributed to purchase a home." I asked, "How much would that be?" He replied, "Let me check."

I was on hold for quite a while. Finally he came back on the phone. "You have $25,000 that you can borrow to purchase the home." I could hardly believe my ears. I replied, "What do I need to do to borrow the $25,000?" He replied, "It will take some time to process forms, but you need to contact your work administrator and they will have the paperwork necessary for submission."

I hung up the phone and went immediately to the Human Resources Department and processed the request form. The check for the $25,000 arrived the day before the closing. Amazingly the sellers had changed their minds and no longer wanted to sell, but we had a signed purchase and sales agreement and I had the funds necessary to purchase the property.

I had prayed for enough money to be able to purchase a home for myself and my Dad, and that prayer had been answered. I praised the Lord for providing me with a home for me and my Dad. After the closing, I went and walked the perimeter of the land, and got down on my knees and dedicated it to the Lord for his service and purpose.

That spring I furnished the home with furniture from second-hand stores and garage sales. My friends from work who had rented by the week were pleased that they had been able to help me acquire the home.

I continued to work and was able to pay off my Fidelity loan as well as to pay for a subdivision of the land making it into three separate lots. The home was then reappraised, and amazingly the value of the home increased.

My extra work allowed me to finish the lower level of the home into an apartment for my Dad. But my Dad was not ready to come to live with me, and my busy work schedule meant I was home just Friday night and Saturday during the day.

Opportunity Knocks

The following spring while I attended a caregiver workshop, I met a woman who had a home on the water that she rented from a summer camp web site. As we talked I realized that I could also rent my home during the summer months until my Dad arrived. I contacted the State of Vermont and obtained a license to use my home as a summer vacation rental and then listed my home on the web and began accepting rentals from June through September.

My first vacation rental season went extremely well. My friends provided me with a place to be on my Friday night off and I used my Saturday from 11 am to 3 pm to clean and get my home ready for the next weekly renter. There was a lot to accomplish in just four hours. Beds needed to be changed, laundry done, fridge and oven cleaned, dishes washed, floors vacuumed and mopped, and the lawn needed to be mowed.

God's Hand

One Saturday, when I traveled to the property I could see large black dark clouds filling the sky. I prayed and asked the Lord to hold back the rain until I mowed the lawn. As I arrived at my home I opened the garage door and went to get the riding mower. As I looked outside large drops of rain began to fall.

I decided I could not mow. As I went to leave the garage, I stopped myself. I looked up to heaven and said, "Lord you are God, you can do anything. This lawn needs to be mowed today. Let it rain everywhere else but not right here. Take your hand and hold it over this property because I am going to mow this lawn."

I then went back into the garage and started the lawn mower. As I exited the garage on the lawnmower large drops of rain started to fall on me and on the lawnmower. I thought to myself this is crazy. But I continued to pray as hard as I could that same prayer and I began to mow the lawn. Amazingly the large drops of rain subsided as I mowed. Every once in a while one, two or three would splatter on the mower and on me.

As I finished the last stretch of lawn that needed to be mowed, suddenly, like a facet that had been turned on, pouring rain came down from the dark clouds. I started laughing as I drove the mower back to the garage. I was soaking wet by the time I got inside the garage. God had indeed held his hand over the property until I had finished mowing that lawn. This was truly amazing. I knew it would be hard for anyone without faith to believe. But not for me -- I knew the Lord could do anything!

A Door Opens

With the subdivision approved, I was advised by a

friend to put up a rental property. A construction loan was acquired. Because I owned the land, no down payment was required to obtain the loan. Within a year, the rental home was finished and I had it rented. I had chosen a house plan with the same layout of the small ranch home that had the possibility for a lower level apartment.

In the end, the value of the entire property was well over ten times the value of the retirement account that I had told the Lord I would not take from my former husband. The Lord had done abundantly above and beyond all that I had asked.

Do What You Can

My extra work allowed me to finish the lower level of that rental property and rent that unit out as well. Through the rental property, the Lord blessed me with many new friends, as well as a home for me and my Dad to live in.

The secret to living an abundant life of faith is in doing everything that you can possibly do to make things happen and asking the Lord for His help. Most people expect things without any effort on their part. But when we drain ourselves and do the absolute best we can, that is when the windows of heaven open in ways that we could never imagine.

Chapter 16

God's Unconditional Love - Hippos

Happy is he that hath the God of Jacob for his help, whose hope is

in the LORD his God. Psalm 146:5

There were delightful surprises contained during the accounting of souls for each had affinities to certain things while they had been on earth. My soul's accounting would include my affinity to hippotamuses as well as the reason why they had become special to me.

After dedicating my life to Christ, I became aware of many flaws in my life. If my life were a garden, it would be as though I became aware of plants I thought were good that were actually weeds. The convicting power of God's Holy Spirit is a purifier and a cleanser, 'scrubba a dub dubbing' our characters to remove those flaws.

Divine Healing

Wounds from childhood criticism surfaced and feelings

related to my worth were challenging to face. My facades were being removed as the Lord began to strip away my sense of security related to intelligence, appearance and material wealth. As this occurred, I prayed and asked the Lord for something to help me understand the love of God. Suddenly I felt God ask me a question, "What do you think is the ugliest animal in the world?" My immediate answer was "A hippopotamus! They are just amazingly ugly, huge, and unattractive!" Without hesitation God responded, "They are beautiful to me!"

This news directly from the Lord made me smile. I suddenly understood. If what I thought was 'ugly' was 'beautiful' to the Lord, then I was beautiful too, with all my flaws and problems. The moment I comprehended God's love, hippopotamuses became my favorite thing. When self-condemning thoughts arose, I would think of hippos and smile. I was loved and God was in control. My job was to listen and obey. The Lord's job was to make all things new.

My First Hippo

The first hippopotamus I ever received was a gift from my husband's sister. It was actually a family of hippos: a papa, a mama and a baby. This family of hippos is one of my favorites and is on a shelf in my home. Other hippopotamuses would follow.

A Courthouse Hippo

One of the most significant hippos I ever received came at a time in my life when I was totally discouraged and distraught. When I got up on that day, I told the Lord, "I need a 'token' from you, something I will recognize immediately as coming from you that can bring me comfort and assurance that you are indeed in control of everything!" I thought no more about it and began my day.

My first stop that day was to the Burlington Courthouse for some court documents I needed. That very morning I had put a small blue case containing nail clippers and scissors into my purse from my suitcase so I could use them more readily.

When I got to the courthouse, the court officer at the check-in station confiscated that blue case. He told me, "You can have it back, but you need to come around to my desk before you leave to pick it up." When I was ready to leave I walked to his desk to pick up my blue case. As I turned to walk out of that courthouse, on the top of the shelf of the police detecting machine I looked and saw what I thought was a hippopotamus. I could hardly believe my eyes!

I walked closer and said, "Do I see a hippopotamus in this courthouse!" The court officer, walked behind me as I walked to see that hippo. "Yes," he replied. I asked, "What is a hippopotamus doing in this court house?" When I got closer, I saw the hippo had a rubber on his nose used for fingers to count pieces of paper. "And what is this rubber doing on his nose?" I asked. I then impulsively walked to the hippo and pulled it off and handed it to the officer. He replied sheepishly as he took the rubber finger from me, "A boy brought that hippo into the court house about three years ago and left it. We have been holding onto the hippo for him to return to get it.

We put the rubber on his nose so that the hippo could catch the rubber bands that we throw at him in our spare time. The rubber bands stick better to his nose with the rubber on." I told the court officer, "This hippo does not like that rubber on his nose!"

Now the court officer looked at me, I could see in his eyes he was thinking, 'What is this woman doing here? She's a 'nut'.' I felt the tables turn as he asked, "What is your great interest in hippos anyway?" Now I was on the 'hot seat' and I replied sheepishly, "Well, I collect them."

Without hesitation the court officer took the hippo in his hand and held it in the air in front of me and said, "Would you like this one?" I was spell bound. I said, "Yes!" I then asked, "You are giving this hippo to me?" He replied, "Yes, you can have him." I left the courthouse and stood on the front step holding my new hippo. Suddenly tears ran down both my eyes. This was the token I had requested from the Lord. Most amazingly a small child had left it there for me three years before, just about the time that the problems with a tenant who was renting from me had started.

The Lord knew that I would have to go to that courthouse. The Lord knew because of the problem, I would ask him for a "token". That hippo had been placed there and had been waiting for me for three years to stop and pick it up!

I put that hippopotamus on the front dash of my car. I had to add sticky tape to his feet to keep him from flying off of the dash when I did sharp turns with the car. But that is where that hippopotamus stays as a reminder to me of the power of the Lord.

I went back to thank that court officer and we became good friends, and I even hired him to help with plumbing, electric, and for other needs.

Hippopotamus in a Tree

Years would pass before I would receive my next special hippo. Once again I was in deep distress emotionally and prayed for the Lord to comfort me. While I was at work that day, I received an email from my sister

Lisa. In the subject line was 'Hippo found in tree!" By now my family knew I liked hippos.

Lisa had gone on a walk looking for her lost dog and had felt the Lord tell her to go down a road she had never been on before. As she walked along the road she spotted something pink in a tree. There were no homes around, so she went to investigate what it was. It was a pink hippopotamus with a heart in its hand. She wrote, "I just knew the hippo was for you, Dawn. It's been in the tree for a long time and it is very dirty, but I will wash it and send it to you."

The day before that hippo arrived, I was in our family barn and noticed a Glenn Campbell CD in my storage area. I remembered that I enjoyed listening to his music. I told the Lord, as I picked up the CD, "Maybe a song on here can comfort me."

Lisa's pink hippo with the heart in its hand arrived in the mail the next day and I was thrilled. I thought this will be my new sleeping hippo. He's small but he will work! I had not had a sleeping hippo since I gave mine to the atheist doctor who received Christ as his savior just before he died.

Divine Connections

The next day was Saturday. I had a day off which was rare in my world. That day, one of my best friends slipped on ice and fell down some outdoor stairs. The emergency attendants called me and asked me to meet her in the emergency room. As I left my home I told the Lord, "I am okay giving up my day off to be with my friend in her hour of need."

As I got into my car I told the Lord, "Well, this would be a good time to see if there is a song on this Glenn Campbell CD to comfort me." As I pushed it the tape and listened to the music, the lyrics from one of his songs made me cry. The song lyrics were: "There is someone walking behind you, Turn around, look at me. There is someone to love and guide you, turn around look at me. Oh I've waited, but I'll wait forever, here's my heart in my hand . . . . .Turn around! Look at me!" I could not help but connect the lyrics of that song with the hippo with the heart in its hand that Lisa had found and mailed to me. These events tied together seamlessly into a divine message of comfort, encouragement and hope.

My friend turned out to be okay. She had pulled muscles in her back but had no broken bones. I realized that the call that requested my help with her injury, had delivered more comfort to me than any sacrifice I thought I had made on my day off to be with her in the emergency room.

The Lord's blessings usually don't come in nicely wrapped packages, but often involve sacrifice and service, sorrow and loss.

A Sleeping Hippo

I brought my new pink hippo to show my friends at a law firm in St. Albans and to tell them the amazing story behind it. After I had told my tale, I commented that he wasn't the best hippo to sleep with, but he would do. One of my friends in the law firm, Julie, immediately told me about a hippo she had seen on the internet designed just for sleeping. As we talked, she did a search and displayed the sleeping hippo on her computer screen. She said, "Come here and see, this is the hippo -- you should buy it, it's not every expensive!" I looked. He was quite the hippo, but I replied, "You don't understand, I don't buy hippos, hippos are given to me. He is a very nice hippo though." I finished visiting and left. As I went down the stairs I said to the Lord, "Well Lord, I really *did* like that hippo, but I don't need another hippo and I am certainly not going to buy him!"

About a week later a box arrived in the mail. Inside the box was that very hippo that Julie had shown to me on the internet. As I opened the gift card that came with it, I expected to see Julie's name on it. I thought how special, Julie must have bought it for me. But the note was not from Julie, it was from my oldest sister! I could hardly believe it.

I picked up the phone immediately and called Julie. I said, "Julie, remember that hippo you showed me?" She said, "Yes." I replied, "Well, I just got it in the mail!" She replied, "No way!" I said, "Yes, my oldest sister sent it to me – I just had to tell you." We were both amazed. I believe the Lord delights in bringing joy in small ways to our lives, especially when we are not expecting anything. I called my oldest sister to thank her for sending the sleeping hippo and told her the amazing story.

A Child's Hippo

One other hippo story occurred when I returned from a flight into Burlington Airport. I had asked the Lord to provide someone who would be willing to give me a ride back to the University so I would not have to use a taxi. The gentleman who sat beside me on my flight back to Burlington volunteered to have his wife and daughter give me a ride to the top of the hill in Burlington where my car was parked. As I got into the back seat with his daughter, she immediately told me, "My name is "Emma" and is spelled, "E -M -M -A!" As she spelled her name, I noticed a pink stuffed toy on the seat that looked like a rabbit. I picked it up and said, "Oh you have a rabbit here!"

But as I looked, I realized it was not a rabbit. It was of all things a hippopotamus! I commented, "Wow, it's not a rabbit, it's a hippopotamus! That's pretty unusual!"

The gentleman turned around to look at me from the front seat and replied with a degree of apology, "Well, Emma just got that yesterday. I know it is a bit odd, but it was a gift to her." I looked at Emma and said, "You know I have one of the smallest hippos in the whole world. It's in my car and I will give one of them to you." Emma held up a small toy rabbit, and asked, "Is it as small as this rabbit?" I looked and assessed the small rabbit. I said, "I believe it will be just the right playmate for your rabbit. It is a little smaller but they can play together."

When we got to my car, the man commented to his wife, as he saw the hippo on my car's dash, "She really does have a hippopotamus!" I got the baby hippo from my car and handed it to Emma through the window. Her eyes widened and her little hands took the small hippo. I said, to the man, "Well, it's pretty small, for her! Hopefully she won't lose it and I hope it does not cause problems for you." I thanked them both for the ride. About a month later I received an email from this gentleman. He hoped he had emailed the right person. He wrote, 'I just want you to know Emma still has that hippo and enjoys it very much."

Meeting this gentleman on the plane and having his daughter Emma receive a gift hippopotamus the day before, was for me just another confirmation of the power of God, and how he can use circumstances to bring us joy and peace.

The Smallest Hippo in the World

The smallest hippo in the world came from a trip I had made to attend a meeting. I had parked on the street and needed coins for the outside parking meter. I entered the store I was parked in front of to get change. At the register, I spotted the small hippos. They were in a display case with many other small delightful animals. I purchased six of the small hippos and put them under my large hippo on my car's dashboard from the court house. Now my car hippo had a family!

The Story Behind Giving Away Small Animals

On December 29, 2010, a friend of mine died who was a bee specialist from Morocco. I remembered seeing bees with all of the small animals and I called the store and purchased two of every one in stock, including several of the small bees. When the bees and the other animals arrived I wrote a letter to the King of Morocco and included one of the small rubber bubble bees as a token in his memory for my friend and his work related to the preservation of bees.

I then wondered what I would do with the rest of the small animals. I prayed about how to use them. It did not take long to have an answer. They were great to give to children for good behavior in stores, and to clerks as a 'thank you' for service. Those small animals now travel with me wherever I go, and are used along with the Bible tracts to brighten the lives of those I meet.

A Man Nicknamed "Hippo"

One example of how those animals can brighten someone's day occurred one morning when I stopped at a fast food restaurant and noticed a man sitting in a truck. I went over to him and told him I had something for him to brighten his day. I then pulled out my little sack of small animals. As I pulled out a rhino, I asked if he had a favorite animal. He replied, "Hippos, do you have a hippo?" I reached back into the bag – the bag was opaque so I could not see through it, but the very next animal I picked out of the bag was a hippopotamus.

The man looked quite amazed as I handed it to him. He said, "My nickname is Hippo." I told him I collected hippos and that they reminded me of the power of the Lord to meet our needs and that I hoped the hippo would remind him of that too. As I walked away, he called me back to his truck, He said, "Wait, come back, I want you to see where the hippo will be riding from now on – on my truck visor." I replied, "That is very cool!" I laughed as I walked back to my car. I mused about the oddity of his nickname being "Hippo" and the fact that a hippo was the second animal I had pulled from that bag! This was just another amazing moment revealing to me, and to him, just how much God cares for us.

The Find the Hippos Game

My home became filled with hippos received from friends. Each room housed at least one, and finding the hippo in the room became a game for visitors. The hippos were been paired with other hippos of the same color to create families of hippos. And anytime I see a hippo, I am reminded of the wonderful power of God.

Chapter 17

Day's Extended

Those on earth who loved the Lord were known in heaven and prayers on their behalf had netted many an unexpected event. I had known several souls that had loved the Lord and had dedicated their life on earth to serve God.

Densmore Drive

One such encounter had happened in September 2004 when I had received a call from a care agency who thought they had an overnight assignment that would work with my schedule. Directions were given to me to visit a woman in Essex Junction, VT. When I arrived, I was interviewed. I was told, "The assignment is not for me, but for my sister, Flo." After the interview, I followed her in my vehicle to her sister's home. As we travelled, she turned onto "Densmore Drive." I was astounded; "Densmore" was my last name. When I got out of my car, I said, "This is my assignment! We are on Densmore Drive!" She replied, "Well, Flo will make that determination." I fell in love with Flo immediately, and I was hired for that position. I was with her six nights each week from 9 pm to 7 am.

I had just enough time to go from my day job that ended at 4:30 pm, to get to my Burlington assignment from 4:30 to 8:30 pm, and travel to Essex to start my 9 pm assignment and go back to my day job for 7:30 am. My assignments were a perfect fit. I was with Flo for almost two years and was with her when she died in the hospital. I was holding her hand when she passed to be with the Lord. I remained friends with her sister until she also died and went to heaven.

The Work Quilt

Almost seamlessly, like different pieces of a quilt, the Lord provided me with another nightly assignment to care for another elderly woman who had taken a fall. When I was told her name, I realized I had met her husband years before. When we met, I had learned her husband had died. I became part of her care giving team six nights a week from 7:30 pm to 7:30 am.

The very first night I was with her, I determined that I would sleep on the floor next to her bed. She was not doing very well, and I wanted to make sure I was there to help her in the night if she needed me. On my first night, we were together in her camp on the lake. As I got ready to go to sleep, I suddenly felt the presence of her husband standing beside me in the room. His energy was unmistakable. I was unsure what to do, but decided that I would not speak to him. But whenever I was with her, I could sense his presence.

Within a few weeks, we moved to her condo in town. As I sat on the couch during my first night in the condo, I felt him sit on the arm of the couch. I felt the couch arm press down as his weight settled on it. This time I spoke to him and said, "I am here to take care of your wife." Eventually I told her that I knew he husband was watching out for her.

My assignment with this woman was just amazing. She was 96 and was still actively engaged with helping people. She loved her family and her many grandchildren visited regularly.

The Life Threatening Illness

I had been with her over a year when she suddenly became ill. The Visiting Nurse Association came and made an assessment and put her on hospice care, as they determined she would not live very long. When I heard of the seriousness of her illness, I prayed, "Lord, I just don't understand this. Here is a woman who at 96 wants to serve you! Why are you taking her home when our world needs laborers so badly? Please intervene! Please don't take her, she wants to live!"

The Divine Message

That night, as I was on the floor at the foot of her bed, my spirit was suddenly pulled out of my body and I was placed sitting at the bottom of her bed. Suddenly her husband appeared right beside me. I could see him perfectly. Without hesitation I reached out to touch him, but my hand and arm went right through him. He looked at me with an expression that said, "Whatever do you think you are doing?" Then he spoke to me and said, "Her days have been extended." He had a leather box in his hand. Now his wife was awake and she sat up in bed behind us and began to talk to him. As she talked, I was suddenly pulled off the bed and found myself hovering at the ceiling in the corner of the room.

I watched, as he handed her the leather box and she excitedly got onto the floor and spread the contents of cards all over the floor that were inside. He joined her on the floor, and they both went through the cards and talked as they looked through them. I watched this happen. Then suddenly I was back in my body at the bottom of the bed.

Her husband was now gone and the woman was also back in bed and stirring. I spoke her name and said, "We have had a visitor." She replied emphatically, "I know that!" I asked, "Your husband brought you cards, what were they?" She replied, "Those weren't cards; they were postcards of all of our travels. They have been missing for a long time! I am so glad he brought them!" I told her, "Well, he told me to tell you, your days have been extended." She asked, "What does that mean?" I replied, "I believe it means you are going to get well, and that your days are extended." She said, "I dreamed I was 97, do you think I will make it to 97?" I replied, "I am not sure; I only know you will get better!" The experience was exhilarating for both of us. It took some time, but finally we both went back to sleep.

Unbelief

In the morning I decided I would let her tell the day caregiver what had happened. When I retuned that night for my night shift, I asked the caregiver if she had been told anything that day. She had not been told. Now I was asked, "What happened?" I replied, "Well, we had a visitor, her husband appeared to both of us last night and told me her days were extended."

My revelation was met with disbelief. "She is on hospice care and she is going to die," was her reply. "No," I replied, "She will get well, I was told her days have been extended!" My response received total disbelief.

She did get well, and the caregiver acknowledged

that I had been right after all. The woman lived another eight months. She did not make it to her 97th birthday, but it was close.

The Passing

I was with her when she passed. She awoke that morning at 4 am with one sneeze. She never sneezed with just one sneeze; she always sneezed in three's. I quickly got up and brought her the medicine that had been prepared and gave it to her. I then sat with her and held her hand and told her how much I loved her. I had to wait 10 minutes before I could administer another dose of the medicine.

As we waited, I sang her the song I had created for her modeled after, *"Mary Had a Little Lamb"*. One of my job requests had been to find fun things that would entertain her. The song had come to me in answer to my prayer to help me to entertain her. So I sang:

"Annie had a Callie cat,

Callie cat, Callie cat;

Annie had a Callie cat

Whose fur was black as coal;

And everywhere Annie went,

Annie went, Annie went;

Everywhere Annie went

That cat was sure to go."

As I sang the last verse, she pulled her chest back to sneeze again. I could see she was going to depart. As our eyes locked, I said, "Please tell Jesus I said hello!" She looked at me with her eyes wide open, and in the next second, she was gone. Callie her faithful cat that she loved dearly, did not go with her. The family asked if I would like to take Callie. I was honored and excited to be able to have the cat and I took her home with me. But as my life continued to involve a lot of overnights, I determined it was best to have my neighbor who loved cats, take her until I could be home nights myself. Callie has since died, but one of my wonderful anticipated moments to come, is getting to see this woman and her husband in heaven when I get there.

Chapter 18

After Death Visitations

Let not your heart be troubled: you believe in God, believe also in me, in my house are many mansions, if it were not so, I would have told you. I go to prepare a place for you, and if I go to prepare a place for you, I will come again, and receive you unto myself, that where I am there you may be also. John 14:1.

Like the iceberg that took down the Titanic, the life accounting was deep and broad and contained information that people had not permitted others to see.

My own soul's accounting would include hidden 'huge secrets' I kept from everyone. Things that I had not believed were possible including the appearances of people to me after they had died.

After Death Appearances

My first appearance from heaven was from Patti Pratt. She joined the church that I attended and we had become best friends. Patti had a husband that was beating her, and with encouragement, she was able to leave him and get a place of her own. She created a beautiful garden and we began to do everything together. As a new Christian she was hungry to know about God's promises contained in the Bible. But Patti was not feeling well, and a trip to her doctor brought some devastating news; she had breast cancer. She quickly arranged to have a mastectomy. In her follow up examination, she was told the operation had been successful, that she was cancer free. But a year later she was not fine. Again not feeling well, she was told her cancer was back and that it had spread to her lymph nodes and to her bones and she had less than six months to live.

Soon Patti could not get out or attend church. She was required to wear a neck brace and was told if she moved her neck, she could become a paraplegic. She was told that her bones were filled with cancer and that it was possible that the weight of her head could break her neck. I began visiting Patti every night after work to fix supper for her and I began to spend Sunday's with her reading and discussing different accounts from the Bible.

We prayed for her healing, but it was soon apparent she would die. She told me, "Live your life, because you just never know what a day will bring forth." She told me that she regretted not wearing clothes to work that she felt were too nice to wear. She said, "Live your life Dawn and don't worry what other people think."

The Announcement

One day she announced to me that she had determined that she would come back to me from heaven after she died. I told her I was pretty sure she would not be allowed to do that. But she insisted, "No, I will come to you." Although I wanted to believe her, I was pretty sure she would not be allowed to do that. But the night that Patti died, she *did* come back to me. She whooshed into my bedroom with her head inside a bubble. Her face came inches from my head, and she told me, 'It's beautiful!" And then she was gone. I cried and thanked her for returning to me and for her confirming the beauty of heaven.

A Second After Death Appearance

My second visitor from heaven was Barbara Ordway. Barbara and I were working together in Burlington. One of her friends was Kay Trudell. Kay had explained the eternal promises of the Bible and of the relevance of the life and death of Jesus Christ to her, but Barbara did not like what was being said. One day she demanded an answer from me as she asked, "Do you believe like Kay Trudell believes?" I replied, "I am afraid I do." Barbara was clearly not happy with either of us. I determined I would pray for her and pray I did -- every day for over a year.

During that year, Barbara was diagnosed with cancer and one day she showed up in the office. This time she demanded that I pray with her. I was startled and told her, "I am not sure I can do that. You told me you do not believe in the work of Jesus Christ, and in order to pray with me, you need to have faith in Jesus and his work on the cross for salvation."

She assured me, "I am ready to pray!" I asked almost in

disbelief, "So you are telling me that you believe that Jesus came, that he was crucified, died and rose from the dead to pay for the sins done in the world?" She replied, "Yes!" I said, "Well, then let's pray!" She repeated a prayer after me, saying, "Lord I believe you died and rose from the dead, and I ask you to forgive me for my sins and remember me when I come into your Kingdom."

When we finished that prayer, she said, "Is that it?" I said, "Indeed it is! For whosoever shall call upon the name of the Lord shall be saved. For salvation is by faith and not of works least any man should boast. For God so loved the world that he gave his only begotten son, that whosoever believeth on him, should not perish but have everlasting life. For the Lord came not to condemn the world, but that the world through him might be saved."

Barbara left that day and died about a month later. The night of the day that she died, she also came to me in a bubble above my bed. When I saw her I said, "Barbara, you are dead!" She ignored me, and reached through the bubble and gave me a hug, and said, "Thank you!"

We both were crying, and then she was gone. I knew at that moment that she *knew* that I had prayed very hard for her and for her family for a very long time. I continued to pray for her family, and sent a note to her husband years later about what happened. When I called to talk with him, He was not surprised and he thanked me for the note and for the call.

A Third After Death Encounter

The third person who had returned to me from heaven was Kevin Smith. He had been in a terrible motorcycle accident and was paralyzed from the waist down. I met him at a fair during his first outing since his accident. He was confined to a wheelchair and was miserable. The day we met, I felt compelled to go and talk with him to find out what had happened. It turned out he lived just around the corner from my home. I began to visit him to help him with dishes, and other things around the house and I shared my faith with him as well.

One day I said, "Kevin, let me ask you something. Had it not been for this accident, would you have even given me the time of day to listen to things about heaven?" His reply was instantaneous, "Absolutely not!" I said, "Did you know that the Bible says that it is better to lose an arm or a leg in this life and enter eternal life maimed, than to enter eternity without the Lord?" He did not know that.

Time passed, and Kevin was not happy. I continued to visit and felt compelled to call him one day. As we talked on the phone, I said, "Kevin, why don't you pray with me. We have known each other now for over three years. You need to get right with God." Kevin did pray with me that day over the phone. I assured him that the Lord could help him, and although he might not walk again, I was sure that the Lord had plans for his life.

Unfortunately, without my knowing, Kevin had already planned to take his life. Within a few days of my call, I got a call from one of my sisters who informed me that he had taken his life. I knew Kevin was in heaven. When I hung up the phone that day, I talked to Kevin and told him I thought it was unfortunate that he had done that, and I was sure if he had to do it over, he would not have taken his life. I was sure he now could see things differently.

The night of the day he died, while I was on an assignment with a woman I got up in the middle of the night. As I looked out the window at all of the stars, I thought about eternity. Suddenly, as I looked at the stars, I heard Kevin speak to me. His distinctive accent highlighted the words as he spoke, "You have no idea how **vast** it is!" I replied, "Kevin, I know you are with the Lord, thank you for coming and telling me that!"

A Fourth After Death Divine Encounter

The fourth person who had returned to me from heaven was an amazing retired engineer. He had Parkinson's disease that inhibited his ability to speak. As I cared for him, I realized he could communicate with me through his eyes. Somehow I knew when he looked at me, what he wanted and what he was saying.

One day we took a walk out to his park bench that overlooked the lake. As we sat together on the bench, I asked, "Do you know where you will go when you die?" He quickly shook his head "No." I said, "Would you like to have some assurance of heaven?" He shook his head "Yes". As we sat together, I talked to him about Jesus and shared this Bible verse with him:

These things have I written unto you that believe on the name of the Son of God, that ye may **KNOW** that you have eternal life, and that ye may believe on the name of the Son of God. And this is the confidence that we have in him, that if we ask anything according to his will, he heareth us; and if we know that he hear us, whatsoever we ask, we know we have the petitions that we desire of him. (1 John 5:13-15)

I asked him if he would like to say a prayer with me. He nodded his head, "Yes." As I started to pray, he actually spoke and repeated the words after me. That was amazing because he had problems articulating words and rarely spoke. When we finished that simple prayer, I told him I would surely see him on the other side.

It was several months before he became unable to eat. His food was going down the wrong way. He was put on hospice care and I visited him one last time before he died. I told him it had been an honor for me to be able to be with him and that I would continue to pray for him.

Before he died, he came to me in his spirit. He was scared. I was sure he was being attacked by demons. I prayed hard that the Lord would intervene for him as he had done for me. The next day, I learned that he had died. The very next night I had a dream. He came to visit me and he had a friend with him that I did not recognize.

As I looked at him, I said, "I know this is a dream, but I know this is <u>more</u> than a dream. I know you are coming to talk to me." He went to take a step forward to come to me, but the man with him blocked him from moving towards me. He looked at me with his eyes. I knew what he was saying to me. He wanted me to pray for his family, to talk to people, to be more vocal! There was urgency in his eyes. I told him, "I understand." As I looked around him, an angel came down and extended his hand out to me. I reached up to touch the angel's hand. I said to the angel, "I know this is not a dream!" As I turned, another angel appeared and reached down and touched my hand, and then another." Three angels total. I opened my eyes and said, "Thank you Lord so much, please help me to do what I need to do!"

The next day I went online and purchased tracts from the Tract League in Michigan. After my divorce I had stopped giving out tracts because my life was in such a whirlwind. Now I began praying and looking for opportunities to offer them to people. The first ones I gave out, I gave in memory of this amazing man. Truly his urgency reflected the importance for true believers to redeem the time left on earth before the Lord's return, and to pray to the Lord that he would send laborers into the harvest.

God's Use of the Smallest of Things

My experiences interacting with people with the tracts and

small animals were amazing.

On a return flight from the Atlanta airport, I encountered several servicemen on their way to Iraq. I thanked each of them and shared with them the small animals and Bible tracts. One soldier went out of his way to come to meet me along a roped barrier. As I thanked him for his service to America, I handed him a small animal and a tract. He had tears in his eyes and said, "I have something for you as well." He reached into his pocket and pulled out a small folded American flag. Tears were in my eyes as we embraced. As he left, I continued to walk towards my gate. A security officer walked over to me and said, "That is one of the most touching things I have ever seen." As she spoke, I handed her my favorite poem, and a small animal and a tract as well.

The Bear

I remembered too, another amazing experience occurred after giving blood at the Red Cross Center. I was directed to a table where an older man was seated. A volunteer came to me at my table and asked what I would like to drink. Her name was the same as my mother's, so I gave her an animal in memory of my Mom. As I gave her a poem and tract, the older man seated next to me asked, "You wouldn't by chance have a bear?"

Amazingly, I had stopped just the day before at a store and had purchased a bear. I said, "In fact, I do!" As I handed him the bear, he got quiet and said, "I just had bear visit my deck on Sunday. My son has died, and we will have a memorial service this coming Saturday for him. My son loved bears, and I feel the bear that came to us was sent by God."

I assured him that indeed God was definitely attempting to comfort him through the use of bears. I said, "Consider this small bear as a token reminder from the Lord of His everlasting promises and that your son is in heaven looking out for you down here."

Chapter 19

The Rapture

For if we believe that Jesus died and rose again, even so them also which sleep in Jesus will God bring with Him. For this we say unto you by the word of the Lord, that we which are alive and remain unto the coming of the Lord shall not prevent them which are asleep; for the Lord himself shall descend from heaven with a shout, with the voice of the archangel, and with the trumpet of God, and the dead in Christ shall rise first; then we which are alive and remain shall be caught up together with them in the clouds to meet the Lord in the air; and so shall we ever be with the Lord, Wherefore comfort one another with these words. 1 Thessalonians 4 14-18

Even as life on earth obeyed natural laws, there were spiritual laws on earth as well and those who had devoted their lives to serve the Lord were privy to divine secrets while they were on earth. My own accounting would include my amazing experience of one of the promises contained in the

Bible in real time, of how divine justice would be imposed throughout the entire earth in a twinkle of an eye.

For me, one of the most challenging accounts to believe in the Bible involved the return of Jesus Christ with his angels in the air to remove believers from the earth. After Jesus had resurrected from the dead, he was seen for forty days speaking of the things pertaining to the kingdom of God. The last time Jesus was seen on earth was by approximately 500 people on the Mount of Olives where he gave the great commission for believers to be witnesses to the uttermost parts of the earth. Then Jesus was taken up and a cloud received him out of their sight.

And while they looked steadfastly toward heaven as he went up, behold two men stood by them in white apparel; which also said, "Ye men of Galilee why stand ye gazing up into heaven? This same Jesus, which is taken up from you into heaven, shall so come in like manner as ye have seen him go into heaven. (Acts 1: 9-11)

I had struggled with the reality of these verses most of my life. One day I was honest with the Lord and told him how I felt, "This seems just too amazing to be real. How can this possibly happen?" The Lord had answered my question in a truly unexpected way.

A Trumpet Sounds

One morning after caring for an elderly man on an overnight assignment, I had gotten up early as I usually did to read my Bible and to get ready to leave to go to my full time job. As I finished getting ready, I put on my coat to get ready to leave. As I did, I heard the sound of trumpets and singing outside. I wondered what was going on. It was the dawn of the day, and I determined I would go to the window to look and see exactly what was happening outside. As I started to go to the window, I placed my hands in my coat pockets to straighten my coat. As I removed my right hand from the pocket, a small piece of paper fell onto the floor.

As I reached down to pick it up, before I could stand back up, I was pulled right up into the air and through the ceiling into the sky outside. Now I was above homes in the sky! I looked around and could see many other people in the air. We were surrounded by angels positioned in between us in the air. I thought, "Oh my God! This **IS** the Rapture!" I felt sick inside as I thought about those left behind on earth and the predicted seven year tribulation period that would follow.

Then suddenly I was back inside the house and waves of energy were shooting through me from the tip of my head to my toes going back and forth like lightening inside of me. The energy caused my body to jump uncontrollably up and down, over and over again high up off the floor. My heart was racing and my body was extremely hot. My mind tried to process what had just happened. My spirit had been divinely transported in a mock rapture. My questions about the reality of the rapture were over. Jesus told the apostles when he was on earth:

But of that day and hour knoweth no man, no, not the angels in heaven, but my Father only. But as the days of Noah were, so shall also the coming of the son of man be. For as in the days that were before the flood they were eating and drinking, marrying and giving in marriage, until the day that Noah entered into the ark, and knew not until the flood came and took them all away so shall also the coming of the Son of man be. Then shall two be in the field, the one shall be taken and the other left. Two women shall be grinding at the mill, the one shall be taken and the other left. Watch therefore for ye know not what hour your Lord doth come. . <u>Therefore be ye also ready for in such an hour as ye think not the Son of man cometh.</u> (Matthew 24: 37- 44)

The world's unparalleled events mirror what Jesus said would exist before his return to the earth. When the apostles asked, "When shall these things be? And what shall be the sign of thy coming and of the end of the world? Jesus responded:

Take heed that no man deceive you. For many shall come in my name saying, I am Christ, and shall deceive many. And ye shall hear of wars and rumors of wars, see that ye be not troubled: for all these things must come to pass, but the end is not yet. For nation shall rise against nation, and kingdom against kingdom, and there shall be famines, and pestilences, and earthquakes, in diverse places. All these are the beginning of sorrows. Then shall they deliver you up to be afflicted and shall kill you and ye shall be hated of all nations for my name's sake.

And then shall many be offended, and shall betray one another, and shall hate one another. And many false prophets shall rise and shall deceive many. And because iniquity shall abound the love of many shall was wax cold. But he that shall endure to the end the same shall be saved. And this gospel of the kingdom shall be preached in all the world for a witness unto all nations and then shall the end come. (Matthew 24 4-14)

Christ foretold that there would be those that would say, 'where is the promise of his coming, for all things continue as they were from the beginning.' However, the Bible cautions that when the gospel is preached throughout the whole world, and when the cup of inequity is full, **then** shall the end come. Jesus also referred to the season of his coming as a woman ready to give birth, that the birth pains would increase in intensity and frequency and then the end would come. There is a caution in the Bible, "Today is the day of salvation, harden not your hearts."

Truly the return of the Lord in the air for his own will occur **without warning** when it is least expected. He will return when things are quite normal: "men shall be eating and drinking, marrying and given in marriage, and shall know not until the end comes."

Chapter 20

An Audience in Heaven - The Bench

Each soul from generation to generation had waited for the day of the accounting. And each during their wait, were aware of things occurring on earth. Messages were sent to loved ones left behind. Souls who possessed even a small degree of faith were accountable for those experiences as well, even if they had dismissed them as just a coincidence.

Because of the after death visitations in my life, I was very aware that people who had died were able to observe things as they occurred on earth.

An Amazing Man – An Amazing Life

One of the most amazing individuals I ever had the privilege of knowing and working with was Dr. Jean-Guy Beliveau. He was trained to be a civil engineer but he was so much more. He had oversight for the Vermont State MATHCOUNTS Competition, a national challenge sponsored by the President of the United States to encourage middle school students in the many different applications associated with mathematics.

Dr. Beliveau knew how to appreciate each day and was always busy. It was a sad day at the University when news travelled that he had not been feeling well. He had been diagnosed with cancer and had chosen to keep that information as private as possible. Trips were planned for special treatments, but Dr. Beliveau shocked his family when he insisted on purchasing his tombstone.

The University was filled the day we celebrated his life. His wife, Connie, and his four daughters were heartbroken. This family was tight, making their loss more intense. A scholarship was established in his name and a bench was placed at the entrance to Votey Hall, a building he entered for so many years to teach his amazing lessons to students. Rhododendrons were planted on either side of the bench and a plaque was added to it in his memory. After his death, I tried to stay in touch with his family.

Step by Step Faith

Every day as I went to work, his bench at the entrance of the building was a reminder of the value of all that is good.

One day I had arrived at work earlier than usual and needed to swipe my access card to gain entrance to the building. My arms were full of materials. As I placed them down on Dr. Beliveau's bench, to get my swipe card, I noticed weeds were growing in the brick work under the bench. I sighed as I remembered him. Well, I thought, in respect for Jean-Guy, I will start this day by weeding under his bench. As I weeded, I told the Lord, "Let the things in my life that are unpleasing to you, be as easily removed as these weeds." As I worked, I suddenly heard a voice behind me say, "So this is how you start your day now - -weeding a bench?!" I stopped weeding and looked up, "Do you know whose bench this is?" I asked. I recognized the man, but could not remember his name. He replied, "No, I do not know whose bench that is!"

I picked up my things off the bench as he opened the door for me, "I am so sorry that I don't remember your name," I said. He replied with his name. I said, "Well, that is Dr. Beliveau's bench and he died about three years ago, he was a good friend of mine and in his honor today, I thought I would weed his bench." The man expressed his condolences and started to walk away. "Wait," I said, "I want to share something with you in memory of Dr. Beliveau who is looking out for us here." I handed him a small animal and the Bible tracts. He said thanks and we parted to do our respective jobs.

About midday I had walked past the door to the main office that was open, and was asked to come inside by the main receptionist who said, "Did you know that Jean-Guy Beliveau is in the newspaper today?" I gasped, "What! He can't be! He's dead!" She said, "He's being remembered by the family today, it's his birthday!" I looked in amazement as she showed me the page in the paper with his big smiling face. His family had posted a Birthday remembrance for him in the paper. I could hardly believe it. I had unwittingly chosen his birthday as the day I would honor him and weed under his bench. I thanked her for bringing this to my attention, and left.

After work, I had called Connie his wife. "You need to know that Jean-Guy is alive and well and looking out for you and all of us," I said as I told her what had happened. She invited me to stop at the camp to talk. I went to the camp that very weekend. As we laughed and visited, we remembered Jean-Guy. His grandchildren loved the small animals I had brought them, as well as the tracts with the Bible verses in memory of their grandfather.

For have an audience in heaven watching over us.

Wherefore seeing we also are compassed about with so great a cloud of witnesses, let us lay aside every weight, and the sin which doth so easily beset us, and let us run with patience the race that is set before us. Hebrews 12:1

Chapter 21

Trust in God - The Hug

Every need had an equal opportunity. In the accounting each soul could see opportunities gained, and opportunities lost producing tears of both joy and sorrow.

My choice to travel that narrow road was always a challenge for me. But I knew that the freedom promised by the world would not produce true freedom, but bondage to things and pleasures of this life. Each day I strove to actively choose to serve the spirit and not the flesh. Though my decision to serve Christ was made many years ago, every day that decision had to be reaffirmed and put into practice.

To whom much is given, of him shall much be required. (Luke 12:45)

During the times when much was being required, I had felt like I needed a hug. On one of those days I actually verbalized my need to the Lord. That day, as I got ready to go to work I said right out loud, "Lord, today I could really <u>use</u> a hug! Not a pansy hug, but a hug from someone powerful and strong, someone that makes me know things will be fine." It was a spoken need, but I had no expectation of having it actually fulfilled. My intent had been to just be honest with the Lord about my needs.

The Dream

That day was very busy and when I got home, I was in bed by 7:30 pm and soon after I went to sleep. I instantly dreamed a dream that was so real I would have sworn that it had really happened.

In the dream I was driving a huge truck and was following a tractor with two men on it on a road that was wet.   The tractor in front of me stopped quickly and unexpectedly. When I applied the truck brakes, it caused the truck to jackknife and then to go backwards off the road into a very large liquid manure pit. The cab of the truck filled quickly with liquid manure. I screamed as the manure rose to the level of my neck, "Get me out of here!

Please, get me out of here!"

The two men on the tractor rushed over and managed to get me out of the truck and then hosed off. My clothes were no longer wearable, so they were thrown away. Now I stood totally naked. One of the men tried to hide his laughter, as he walked me to the corner of a house where I sat down.

I curled up with my arms around my legs under a large tree and waited for him to return with clothes for me to wear. As I sat, I talked to myself, "It's a beautiful day! You are not hurt, you'll have some clothes soon and you'll be on your way!" I felt better.

The house was situated on top of a large hill and overlooked a field. The sky was deep blue. I waited and watched as cars passed on a road in front of me.

The Rider and Chariot

Suddenly in the sky I saw a white horse with a chariot and a driver galloping through the blue sky. The driver wore a cape that blew in the wind behind him. The reins on the horse were gold and there was gold on the chariot too.

It was so exciting to see this happening. I wondered, "Can the people in the cars see them too?" As I watched the horse galloping through the air, the rider and chariot began to do a large turn and was coming my way. I realized if I stood away from the house, I would be able to see them up close.

Quickly I moved away from the house and positioned myself so I could watch for them. Sure enough, the horse with the chariot and driver were headed my way, but as they approached, they disappeared behind the limbs and leaves of a large tree right next to the house. I stood and waited and watched. They had to come out the other side of the tree and I had a perfect view!

Then to my amazement as I watched, the white horse, chariot and driver came out from behind the tree and turned again. They came right over the top of the roof of the house and the chariot landed right beside me. I could hardly believe my eyes!

The driver was now right beside me on the ground. He quickly put his arms around me and held me tightly. His arms circled my back as he gave me a strong hug. I said, "Oh please, please take me with you! Please let me go with you in your chariot now!" Then I opened my eyes to look at him, but suddenly he was gone as well as the horse and the chariot that had been right there! It had been a 'dream', but I could feel his arms still on my back, as though he was still right there with me, giving me that hug.

I remembered my request to the Lord that very morning, and I thanked the Lord for what had just happened. The image of the white horse and the rider remained seared into my mind. Some things cannot be explained. This was one of those things.

A framed picture

About a month later, one of my sisters handed me a small framed picture that contained a similar scene of a deep blue sky with a field and houses. The only thing missing was the chariot and the driver in that picture. I hung that picture at the entrance to my home as a daily reminder that the Lord is indeed in control. *Enter in at the narrow gate: for wide is the gate, and broad is the way, that leads to destruction, and many there be who go in there at: Because straight is the gate, and narrow is the way, which leadeth unto life, and few there be that find it.* Matthew 7:14

Chapter 22

The Reality of Angels

The accounting revealed many bad things had been allowed to happen to good people. The books that most appropriately placed beside each other in the Bible are *Job* and *Psalms.* The book of *Job* is placed before the book of *Psalms*, and that seems appropriate to me because it is through suffering that we have the opportunity to praise His Holy Name.

Angels

Among the most widely discussed topics on earth is the subject of angels. Depicted in programs, movies, and used by the media for entertainment, the reality of their existence is hotly debated. For those who walk with the Lord, the reality of angels is not in question. During the accounting, souls gave accounts of prayers for the Lord to provide His angels to protect them from the demons on earth who were allowed to generate problems.

Job's encounter with Satan had always caused me to plead with the Lord for His protection. The account goes as follows:

Now there was a day when the sons of God came to present themselves before the Lord and Satan came also among them. And the Lord said unto Satan, "Whence comest thou?" Then Satan answered the Lord, and said, "From going to and fro in the earth, and from walking up and down in it? And the Lord said unto Satan, "Hast though considered my servant Job, that there is none like him on the earth, a perfect and an upright man, one that feareth God, and eschewed evil?

Then Satan answered the Lord, and said, "Doth Job fear God for naught? Hast thou not made a hedge about him, and his house, and about all that he hath on every side? Thou hast blessed the work of his hands, and his substance is increased in the land. But put forth thine hand now, and touch all that he hath and he will curse thee to thy face." And the Lord said unto Satan, "Behold all that he hath is in thy power, only upon himself put not forth thine hand." So Satan went forth from the presence of the Lord. (Job 1: 6-12)

The Bible shows Job as passing the divine test. He remained loyal to God, in spite of the loss of his material wealth and of the pain of intense boils on his body. His response to his trial had proven that he had served God for more than the benefits of material and physical health.

Continually my prayer was for the Lord to protect and intervene daily, and to have mercy. My daily prayer was, "Let it not be said on this day forever in eternity that the power of the enemy was greater than your power to intervene, recover, redeem, deliver and restore us from the snares of the enemy. Please, please, please deliver us from the lusts of the flesh, the lust of the eye, the pride of life, the love of this world: that your house be full and that the praise that is due your holy name be present with you forever more!"

A Visit by Six Angels

This prayer had been answered by the Lord one day

with an actual visitation of six angels.

For close to six months, I had prayed and asked the Lord to protect the students that would be a part of an outreach program. The Friday night prior to students arriving, I went to bed early. My stomach turned and turned, and I did not feel well. I prayed and asked the Lord to help me, "Lord, please calm me down. Please assure of your help and protection; of your ability to intervene and answer my prayers!" On Saturday morning when I awoke and opened my eyes, I saw pink effervescent lights beside my bed in the air. I thought, "What is that! I am just waking up, let me close my eyes, something must be in my eyes to cause me to see this."

I closed my eyes then opened them and looked again. The lights were still there. I had rubbed my eyes and looked closer. Yes, there were definitely bright effervescent pink lights in the upper right corner of the room. I sat up in bed to look closer, and as I did, I noticed out of the corner of my right eye, a second set of effervescent lights.

As I turned my head around to look to see these

effervescent lights, in the corner of my eye, were more lights. Now I turned my head completely around the room. To my utter amazement, around my entire bed, were six sets of effervescent pink lights. I got on my knees and moved to get close to examine these lights.

They appeared to be outlines of heads and shoulders and the lights were as bright as effervescent bright Christmas tree lights. It was morning, the room was not dark, and still the lights were extremely bright and they stayed around me. I had concluded that I was seeing the energy field of six angels. This was God's answer to my prayer. Those six angels were there to guard and protect me. I praised the Lord for His help and for sending me the angels.

I told no one about the angels. On Monday, a package arrived in the mail from a friend. Inside was a stone angel that was made from the very same pink effervescent color, not as bright as the lights, but the exact same color! I cried when I opened the package. I had placed the angel on top of my computer monitor at work as a reminder of the power of the

Lord to hear and answer my prayers.

That year, we had one of the most exceptional programs ever experienced. None of the student participants experienced any problems, and it was my first year in 20 years that the staff nurse did not have any trips to the doctor's.

Wherefore seeing we also are compassed about with so great a cloud of witnesses, let us lay aside every weight, and the sin which doth so easily beset us, and let us run with patience the race that is set before us, looking unto Jesus the author and finisher of our faith; who for the joy that was set before him endured the cross, despising the shame, and is set down at the right hand of the throne of God. (Hebrews 12:1-2)

Chapter 23

A Gift from God

The world is full of incredible detail. So it came as no surprise to find during the accounting that details mattered in the spiritual realm. Details were the way excellence was achieved, and details not paid attention to, or overlooked, usually were involved when things went wrong.

My accounting would include answered prayers that had come through paying attention to details.

Each year before Christmas, I would begin a search for something special to present to the Lord for His birthday. What I would give to the Lord would involve something that was not required of me that I believed would bring him joy. And each year, without fail, the Lord had returned a special gift to me as well.

God's Christmas Gift

My account would include one of the gifts the Lord had

returned to me that had been incredibly special. I had just completed a large program and had decided to stop at a local restaurant for dinner before heading home. As I received my meal and began to eat, my favorite song, "The Drummer Boy" began playing in the restaurant. I sat and listened to the lyrics of the song:

Come they told me, pa rum pum pum pum
A new born King to see, pa rum pum pum pum
Our finest gifts we bring, pa rum pum pum pum
To lay before the King, pa rum pum pum pum,
rum pum pum pum, rum pum pum pum,

So to honor Him, pa rum pum pum pum,
When we come.

Little Baby, pa rum pum pum pum
I am a poor boy too, pa rum pum pum pum
I have no gift to bring, pa rum pum pum pum
That's fit to give the King, pa rum pum pum pum,
rum pum pum pum, rum pum pum pum,

Shall I play for you, pa rum pum pum pum,
On my drum?

Mary nodded, pa rum pum pum pum
The ox and lamb kept time, pa rum pum pum pum
I played my drum for Him, pa rum pum pum pum
I played my best for Him, pa rum pum pum pum,
rum pum pum pum, rum pum pum pum,

Then He smiled at me, pa rum pum pum pum
Me and my drum.

As the song played, people one-by-one began to sing along inside the restaurant. I thanked the Lord for the special sacred moment of hearing my song and of having others sing along. When I had finished my meal and was leaving, a couple entered the restaurant with a baby carrier with a newborn child.

I passed them just as the mother placed the baby carrier on a table near the exit. I congratulated them and wished them the best for Christmas. I was excited to see a newborn on the heels of hearing the, 'pa rum pum pum pum' song just before they arrived. Suddenly the newborn child turned its head and looked at me and smiled! As I left the restaurant, I thanked the Lord for His wonderful Christmas present. I told the Lord, "Truly I have played my best for you, Happy Birthday, Jesus!"

"And when they came into the house, they saw the young child with Mary his mother, and fell down, and worshiped him: and

when they had opened their treasures, they presented unto him

gifts; gold, and frankincense, and myrrh." Matthew 2:11

Chapter 24

Iniquity Will Have an End

The accounting proved the promises of God in the Holy Bible were all true. God was not a respecter of persons and was available to everyone. "In Him" we lived and moved and had our being. Anyone who had sought Him with *all* their heart, had found Him and He had honored those that had sought Him. On earth, everything had proven to be temporary. In heaven, everything was eternal.

Scaffolding

The material world had been used by God to prepare souls for eternity. Like 'scaffolding' used to build a building, the purpose of life had not been in the 'scaffolding' -- the acquisition or possession of material wealth or in the pleasures of the body – but rather the material world provided souls with opportunities to acquire the fruit of the Spirit.

But the fruit of the Spirit is love, joy, peace, longsuffering, gentleness, goodness, faith, meekness, temperance, against such there is no law. (Galatians 5: 22-23)

It was through life's trials, sorrows and losses that we had the opportunity to gain spiritual lessons. God was just: sorrows and losses had eternal rewards. Injustices on earth provided "divine dividends' in heaven, and had indeed transformed even the worst life experiences into unique manifestations of God's true power to overcome evil.

The Lord is not slack concerning his promise, as some men count slackness; but is longsuffering toward us, not willing that any should perish, but that all should come to repentance. (2 Peter 3:9)

Life's Choices

'Holy things' done for 'feel good' reasons, lost rewards; and there was judgment for things that could have been done but had **not** been done. Each circumstance had contained the opportunity to exercise: Chastity or lust, temperance or gluttony, charity or greed, diligence or sloth, patience or wrath, kindness or envy, humility or pride. The good news was there was one person who held the key to divine forgiveness, who had paid the price in blood for all of the sins of the world: Jesus Christ.

For God so loved the world, that he gave His only begotten Son, that whosoever believeth in Him, should not perish but have everlasting life. For God sent not his Son into the world to condemn the world, but that through Him the world might be saved. *(John 3:16)*

For without the shedding of blood, there is no remission of sins. (Hebrews 9:22)

To inherit eternal life, each soul was searched for a specific time and date when they had looked to Christ and had acknowledged and asked for forgiveness through His work of redemption. To do that, each soul had to believe the Bible account that Jesus Christ *willingly* died for the sins of the whole world and was resurrected from the dead. Believing alone did not provide salvation, for devils also believed and trembled. It was when Jesus was asked, in faith, to forgive transgressions that the miracle of being 'born again' occurred. In that moment the 'switch' on the light got turned on and that name got written in God's book of life in heaven!

Grace

For by grace are ye saved through faith; and that **not** of yourselves: it is the gift of God: **Not of works**, **lest any man should boast.** *(*Ephesians 2: 8-9)

How shall we escape, if we neglect so great a salvation; which at the first began to be spoken by the Lord, and was confirmed unto us by them that heard him? (Hebrews 2:3)

And ye shall know the truth, and the truth shall set you free. (John 8:32)

What is the truth? The truth is the lust of the flesh, the lust of the eye, the pride of life, the love this world cannot deliver eternal life, and neither can good works. The world is like a maze that has a beginning and an end. Within that maze are many paths, but there is only one path that can set us free. That path is salvation through Jesus Christ whereby we can experience the power of His Holy Spirit in our lives, find peace even in the midst of trials, and experience His joy on earth; and soon: His eternal rewards.

Heaven was, in fact, full of children! Jesus called a child to Himself and set him before them, and said, "Truly I say to you, unless you are converted and become like children, you will not enter the kingdom of heaven." (Mathew 18:2-3)

During the accounting, soul's that had reached accountability on the basis of their ability to make moral choices were aware of the wrongs done during their time on earth. for all have sinned and come short of the glory of God. (Romans 3:23)

Souls that did NOT accept the gift of eternal life through Jesus Christ, were overwhelmed when they heard the words: Depart from me ye that work iniquity, I never knew you. For neither is there salvation in any other, for there is none other name (other than the name of Jesus Christ) given under heaven among men whereby we must be saved. (Acts 4:12)

Therefore whosoever heareth these sayings of mine, and doeth them, I will liken him unto a wise man, which built his house upon a rock. And the rain descended and the floods came, and the winds blew, and beat upon that house; and it fell not; for it was founded upon a rock. And every one that heareth these sayings of mine, and doeth them not, shall be likened unto a foolish man which built his house upon the sand: And the rain descended and the floods came, and the winds blew and beat upon that house; and it fell; and great was the fall of it. (Matthew 7: 24-27)

Not everyone that saith unto me, Lord, Lord, shall enter into the kingdom of heaven; but he that doeth the will of my Father, which is in heaven. Many will say to me in that day, Lord, Lord, have we not prophesied in thy name? And in thy name have cast out devils? And in thy name done many wonderful works? And then will I profess unto them, I never knew you: depart from me, ye that work iniquity. (Matthew 7:21-23)

I tell you, nay: but, except ye **repent**, ye shall all likewise perish. (Luke 13:5)

He that saith, I know him, and keepeth not his commandments, is a liar, and the truth is not in him. (1 John 2:4)

Jesus Christ and his precious Holy Spirit were the 'engine' that moved us forward, and through Him each could experience His abundant life. Virtues <u>followed</u> salvation like a 'caboose.' It was ***after*** one had accepted Jesus Christ with the faith of a child, that one experienced His Amazing Grace:

Amazing grace,
How sweet the sound that saved a wretch like me,
I once was once was lost,
But now I'm found, was blind, but now I see.

Twas grace that taught my heart to fear,
And grace my fears relieved,
How precious did that grace appear
The hour I first believed.

My chains are gone, I've been set free,
My God, my Savior has ransomed me,

And like a flood His mercy reigns
Unending love, Amazing Grace.

The Lord has promised good to me,
His word my hope secures,
He will my shield and portion be
As long as life endures

The earth shall soon dissolve like snow,
The sun forbear to shine,
But God who called me here below will be forever mine, will be
forever mine. You are forever mine!

Everything is Possible

I recalled reading a book entitled, *"The Secret"* that declared 'everything is possible, nothing is impossible' and focused on controlling the power within. Although when these principles were applied, they produced results, they did not contain the message of Jesus Christ. Christ referred to this as, "climbing up some other way." Jesus had also had the opportunity to manifest his own reality and to have whatever he desired during his time on earth, but he did **not**. His mission and goal was **only** to do the Will of His Father.

And the devil, taking him up into a high mountain, showed unto him all the kingdoms of the world in a moment of time. And the devil said unto him, <u>All this power </u>will I give thee, and the glory of them; for that <u>is delivered unto me</u>; <u>and to whomsoever I will I give it</u>; If thou therefore wilt worship me, <u>all</u> shall be thine. And Jesus answered and said unto him, "Get thee behind me Satan: for it is written, thou shalt worship the Lord thy God, and him only shalt thou serve. (Luke 4:5)

That 'power' was indeed still available on earth to <u>anyone</u> who worshiped at the altar of the material world. The accounting revealed the true measure within each soul. Life was not about what we had looked like, or about our material wealth, it had been what was contained within the heart.

We each have freedom to do whatever we want whenever we want, but serving the 'body' without regard for the soul has consequences; bondage to self, loneliness, and isolation.

For the mystery of iniquity doth already work ... Even him, whose coming is after the working of Satan with all power and signs and lying wonders -- with all deceivableness of unrighteousness in them that perish because they received not the love of the truth, that they might be saved. And for this cause God shall send them a strong delusion, that they should believe a lie. (2 Thessalonians 2:7-11)

If ye believe in God, believe also in me, in my Father's house are many mansions. If it were not so, I would have told you. I go to prepare a place for you that where I am, there ye may be also. John 14:1

Chapter 25

Freedom of Choice

These things I have spoken unto you, that in me you might have peace. In the world you shall have tribulation: but be of good cheer; I have overcome the world. John 16:33

Eye has not seen, nor ear heard, neither have entered into the heart of man, the things which God has prepared for them that love him. 1 Corinthians 2:9

Jesus willingly died on a cross and then rose from the dead to save us from the nature we were born with that causes us to want everything to go our way. He did **_not_** promise a life free from trials and sorrows, rather he asks each to pick up 'his cross" and to follow Him. He *did* promise to **_never_** leave nor forsake us.

Peace I leave with you, my peace I give unto you: not as the world gives, give I unto you. Let not your heart be troubled, neither let it be afraid. (John 14:27)

Jesus promised He would return to the earth in the air for his own when we least expect it.

As it was in the days of Noah, so shall it be also in the day of the Son of man. They did eat, they drank, they married wives, they were given in marriage, until the day that Noah entered into the ark, and the flood came, and destroyed them all. Likewise also as it was in the days of Lot, they did eat, they drank; they bought, they sold, they planted, they builded. But the same day that Lot went out of Sodom it rained fire and brimstone from heaven, and destroyed them all. Even thus shall it be in the day when the son of man is revealed. Whosoever shall seek to save his life shall lose it; and whosoever shall lose his life shall preserve it.

I tell you in that night there shall be two men in one bed, the one shall be taken and the other shall be left. Two women shall be grinding together; the one shall be taken, and the other left. Two men shall be in the field, the one shall be taken and the other left. (Luke 17:26-36)

But the day of the Lord will come as a thief in the night; in which the heavens shall pass away with a great noise, and the elements shall melt with fervent heat, the earth also and the works that are therein shall be burned up. (2 Peter 3:10)

But of that day and hour knows no man, no, not the angels of heaven, but my Father only. (Matthew 24:36)

For when they shall say, Peace and safety; then sudden destruction cometh upon them, as travail upon a woman with child; and they shall not escape. (1 Thessalonians 5:3)

Watch therefore: for ye know not what hour your Lord doth come. Therefore be ye also ready: for in such an hour as ye think not the Son of man cometh. Who then is a faithful and wise servant, whom his Lord hath made ruler over his household, to give them meat in due season. Blessed is that servant whom his Lord when he cometh shall find so doing. (Mathew 24:42-46)

The harvest is truly plentiful but the laborers are few.

The Question

The question remains. Who will *you* serve today? Who will *you* put first? For, this gospel will be preached throughout the entire world, and THEN 'the end' will come.

The 'end' of what? The end of iniquity: stealing, robbing, lying, cheating, adultery, killing -- the end of 'right' being called wrong and wrong being called 'right'. This sounds wonderful, no more locks on doors necessary. Right! Unfortunately the reign of Jesus Christ cannot begin without the allowance for man to exercise his right to believe in a universal God who has universal power available to all of mankind for peace on earth that does not require Jesus Christ who is believed to be 'just a man'.

What will trigger this? The rapture! Jesus Christ will return to remove believers from the earth. And this will occur without any warning when people shall say, "peace, peace" -- when things are going fine on earth.

What will happen next? A seven year tribulation

period when men will finally be able to exercise complete FREEDOM without divine restraint. That freedom will create the worst time on earth that has ever happened. The presence of the God's Holy Spirit will have been removed from the earth and there will be no protection from the forces of evil.

What will all of this look like? The Bible says that if God had not shortened the days when this occurs no flesh would survive. There will be miracles of amazing things and those miracles will deceive many. Satan, the chief fallen angel, will be allowed to rule and reign over men with all deceivableness and lying wonders. The fallen angels and demons will have free access to attack whoever they desire. God will still hear prayers in heaven, and men will surely still be saved, but they will experience great persecution for their faith like never before. This tribulation period will last for seven years.

Why this book now? The reason (although no man knows the day or hour) is 'the season' of the Lord's return in the air for his own is suddenly upon us. If you cannot remember a time when you have said, "Lord Jesus, I believe you died for my sins, rose from the dead, and are alive forever in heaven: forgive me and remember me when I come into your Kingdom", I suggest you say that prayer 'today' out loud. Then write the date down in your Bible, sign your name to it and begin reading the Bible.

Now is the accepted time; behold, now is the day of salvation. (2 Corinthians 6:2)

We are admonished: Let not thy heart envy sinners but be thou in the fear of the lord all the day long. For surely there is an end and thy expectation shall not be cut off. (Prov. 23:17)

We are encouraged: To grow in grace, and in the knowledge of our Lord and Savior Jesus Christ. To him be glory both now and forever. Amen. (2 Peter 3:18)

We are assured: If my people, who are called by my name, shall humble themselves, and pray, and seek my face, and turn from their wicked ways; then will I hear from heaven, and will forgive their sin, and will heal their land. (2 Chronicles 7:14)

The Lord Jesus Christ is preparing the earth for His return, even as the Prince of this world, the fallen angel, Lucifer is preparing to rule the earth with his illusion of oneness through universal thought, miracles, and signs – a spiritual counterfeit message that will bring peace on earth for a time but Lucifer's reign will create more war, *not less* as he will promise. Ultimately his reign will culminate with the return of Jesus Christ to the earth to stop the battle of Armageddon and to end the rule of iniquity on earth.

Jesus Christ came to do His Father's will -- **not** his own:

I danced in the morning when the world was young
I danced in the moon and the stars and the sun
I came down from heaven and I danced on the earth
At Bethlehem I had my birth

Dance, dance, wherever you may be
I am the lord of the dance, said he
And I lead you all, wherever you may be
And I lead you all in the dance, said he

I danced for the scribes and the Pharisees

They wouldn't dance, they wouldn't follow me
I danced for the fishermen James and John
They came with me so the dance went on

Dance, dance, wherever you may be
I am the lord of the dance, said he
And I lead you all, wherever you may be
And I lead you all in the dance, said he

I danced on the Sabbath and I cured the lame
The holy people said it was a shame
They ripped, they stripped, they hung me high
Left me there on the cross to die

Dance, dance, wherever you may be
I am the lord of the dance, said he
And I lead you all, wherever you may be
And I lead you all in the dance, said he
I danced on a Friday when the world turned black
It's hard to dance with the devil on your back
They buried my body, they thought I was gone
But I am the dance, and the dance goes on

Dance, dance, wherever you may be
I am the lord of the dance, said he
And I lead you all, wherever you may be
And I lead you all in the dance, said he

They cut me down and I leapt up high
I am the life that will never, never die
I'll live in you if you'll live in me
I am the Lord of the dance, said he

Dance, dance, wherever you may be
I am the lord of the dance, said he

And I lead you all, wherever you may be
And I lead you all in the dance, said he.

Sydney Carter – 1967 Lord of the Dance

Truth Established

Within our modern courts of law, truth is established through two or three witnesses. The Bible contains accounts from a variety of people from all walks of life who witnessed and recorded what they heard Jesus say and do. Many who believed and followed Jesus Christ died terrible deaths because they were unwilling to deny what they had seen and heard. Even the disciple Thomas who doubted Christ's resurrection ultimately believed.

The other disciples therefore said unto him, 'We have seen the Lord.' But (THOMAS) he said unto them, except I shall see in his hands the print of the nails, and put my finger into the print of the nails, and thrust my hand into his side, I will not believe. (John 20:25)

Then Jesus appeared (to the eleven disciples) in the upper room and said: 'Behold my hands and my feet, that it is I myself: handle me, and see; for a spirit has not flesh and bones, as you see me have. (Luke 24:29)

Thomas answered and said unto him, 'My Lord and my God.' (John 20:28)

Tears

During each souls accounting, no matter how many wonderful actions, thoughts and deeds appeared on the plus side, each had done selfish things for personal gain, or desire. Amazingly, even souls that had lived dreadful lives, who had sincerely confessed and turned by faith, to Jesus Christ received forgiveness. In the accounting, faith exercised justified souls and cleansed them for eternity. Here, suddenly the work of Jesus Christ on the cross was fully understood. His sacrifice when appropriated had made all things new.

Here, every knee indeed bowed, and every tongue confessed that Jesus Christ was Lord, to the glory of God the Father. Jesus had indeed provided a way for redemption for everyone. No sin committed had been too great for the mercy and forgiveness of Jesus Christ. Here, there were tears of joy as well as tears of sorrow.

When truth is presented it is refuted, accepted, or condemned. A walk in obedience to Jesus Christ means we agree with Him and value what he said. Men's thoughts about truth do not change truth, but the truth changes us. Jesus promised us, "Love never fails." It is through 'faith' that the Lord is able to place into the small cups of our minds the ocean of His love. When we acknowledge the work of Jesus Christ on the cross and ask Him for forgiveness, we enter into oneness with Him.

So shall my word be that goeth forth out of my mouth: it shall not return unto me void, but it shall accomplish that which I please, and it shall prosper in the thing whereto I sent it. (Isaiah 55:11)

It is 'trials' that provide us with the opportunity to acquire the virtues of love.

In all these things we are more than conquerors through him

that loved us. For I am persuaded, that either death, nor life, nor angels, nor principalities, nor powers, nor things present, nor things to come, nor height, nor depth, nor any other creature, shall be able to separate us from the love of God, which is in Christ Jesus our Lord. (Romans 8:37-39)

I beseech you therefore, brethren, by the mercies of God, that ye present your bodies a living sacrifice, holy, acceptable unto God, which is your reasonable service. And be not conformed to this world: but be ye transformed by the renewing of your mind, that ye may prove what is that good, and acceptable, and perfect, will of God. (Romans 12:1-2)

He is no fool who gives up what he cannot keep to gain what he cannot lose. C. Crowder, Spotlight in Faith - Pg. 201

Therefore come out from among them, and be you separate, says the Lord, and touch not the unclean thing; and I will receive you. (2 Corinthians 6:17)

Let us hear the conclusion of the whole matter: fear God and keep his commandments for this is the whole duty of man. For God shall bring every work into judgment, with every secret thing whether it be good, or whether it be evil. (Ecclesiastes 12:14)

Chapter 26

Walk Worthy of God

God is light and in Him is no darkness at all. 1 John 1:5

The set time for each soul's accounting will happen. Right now, each of us still has time to begin again, to turn to God, to accept salvation from Jesus Christ, to seek ways to use our time and talents to serve the King of Kings, and to share the good news of his free gift of salvation before the end of time begins.

God . . . hath in these last days spoken unto us by His son whom He hath appointed heir of all things, by whom He also made the worlds, who being the brightness of His image of His person and upholding all things by the Word of His power, when He hath by himself purged our sins, sat down on the right side of the Majesty on high. (Hebrews 1:2&3)

God will indeed bind up all of our wounds on that day, even those that go deep.

Devotion Rather Than Duty

Our trust needs to be in the living God, not in a denomination or church alliance – it is Christ that provides salvation. Churches are to preach the truth of God's word. Sadly there are churches that provide more entertainment than life changing, heart pounding messages that stir the soul to desire to change and to serve the living God. Christ admonished believers to assemble together for fellowship, prayer, and to learn and gain a comprehensive understanding of biblical truths that allow us to grow in grace and truth. Just as being present in a garage does not make someone a car, and just being present in a church does not mean someone has been 'born again'.

Gaining Courage and Faith

We need to acknowledge our need for God's Holy Spirit through repentance and acceptance of Christ, and then forget those things that are in the past, make restitution where possible, and begin a walk of faith based upon what we do understand. As we grow in our faith we will begin to understand how the Holy Spirit works through people. That understanding will produce within us courage to share our faith.

As we pray and seek God's will and obey His leading there will appear opportunities for us to demonstrate 'brotherly kindness'. Those random acts of kindness produce a sense of true love for ourselves and others. Christ's goal is not to make us into perfect human beings, but rather to perfect our faith so that we will be able to trust Him to work all of our circumstances together for our good.

And we know that all things work together for good to them that love God, to them that are called according to His purpose. (Romans 8:28)

How much love we exhibit toward others, reveals just how much control we have given to God over our lives. We each have a choice. But seek ye first the kingdom of God and His righteousness and all these things shall be added unto you.

(Matthew 6:33)

A New Heart

A new heart also will I give you and a new spirit will I put within you. I will put my spirit within you and cause you to walk in my statutes and ye shall keep my judgments and do them. (Ezekiel 37:26&27)

True happiness in spite of our circumstances is possible because:"

We have an advocate with the Father, Jesus Christ our righteousness and he is the propitiation for our sins and not for ours alone, but for the sins of the whole world. (1 John 2:1&2)

But as many as received him, to them gave He power, to become the sons of God, even to them that believe on His name which were born not of blood (human birth) nor of the will of the flesh (the mind) nor of the will of man (self-reformation), but of God for all who ask (a free gift). (John 1:12&13)

Let us not be weary in well doing for, in due season we

shall reap if we faint not. (Galatians 6:9)

In a little while I will once more shake the heaven and the earth the sea and the dry land. (Haggai 2:5&6)

May God help each of us to choose to seek Him with *all* of our heart -- may each of us on that day, hear Him say: *Well done!*

RESOURCE:

Radio Bible Class (RBC) Ministries is a great resource for understandable and accessible information about Jesus Christ and His Holy Bible. They offer online guidance and a free monthly devotional entitled, *"Our Daily Bread"* that contains encouragement, comfort, and His divine guidance. To learn more on how to be ready for His return, visit: http://rbc.org/

If you enjoyed, "Divine Encounters: The Reality of God, Angels & Demons" and have had similar experiences, I would love to hear from you: Dawndensmore@gmail.com

For more inspiring information visit:

www.GodsAmazingWays.com

ADDITIONAL BIBLE PROMISES

True worshipers shall worship the Father in Spirit and in Truth for the Father seeketh such to worship Him. John 4:23

Without faith it is impossible to please God, because he, who comes to God, must believe that He is, and He rewards those who seek him. Hebrews 11:6

Trust in the LORD with all your heart; and lean not unto your own understanding.

In all thy ways acknowledge him, and he shall direct thy paths. Prov. 3:5-6

Jesus saith unto him, I am the way, the truth, and the life: no man cometh unto the Father, but by me. John 14:6

And ye shall know the truth and the truth shall make you free.

John 8:32

And behold I come quickly and my reward is with me to give to every man according to his work shall be. Rev. 22:12

And whatsoever ye do, do it heartily as to the Lord and not unto men, knowing that of the Lord ye shall receive the reward of the inheritance for ye serve the Lord Jesus.

But he that doeth wrong shall receive for the wrong that he hath done and there is no respect of persons. Colossians 3:23-25

For other foundation can no man lay than that is laid which is Jesus Christ.

Every man's work shall be made manifest for the day shall declare it because it shall be revealed by fire and this fire shall try every man's work of what sort it is.

If any man's work abide which he heath built thereupon, he shall receive a reward.

If any man's work shall be burned, he shall suffer loss, but he himself shall be saved yet, so as by fire. Know yet not that ye are the temple of God and that the spirit of God dwelleth in you? 1

Corinthians 3: 13-16

By faith, Moses . . . refused to be called the son of Pharaoh's daughter, choosing rather to suffer affliction with the people of God then to enjoy the pleasures of sin for a season, esteeming the reproach of Christ greater riches than the pleasures in Egypt for he had respect unto the recompense of the reward. Hebrews 24:26

And I saw thrones and they sat upon them, and judgment was given unto them, that were beheaded for the witness of Jesus, and for the word of God, and which had not worshipped the beast neither his image, neither had received his mark upon their foreheads, or in their hands, and they lived and reigned with Christ a thousand years.

But the rest of the dead lived not again until the thousand years were finished, This is the first resurrection.

Blessed and holy is he that hath part in the first resurrection on such the second death hath no power but they shall be priests of God and of Christ and shall reign with him a thousand years. Rev 20: 5&6

And I saw a great white throne and him that sat upon it from whose face the earth and the heaven fled away and there was found no place for them.

And I saw the dead small and great stand before God and the books were opened and another book was opened which is the book of life and the dead were judged out of those things that were written in the books according to their works.

And the sea gave up her dead which were in it and death and hell delivered up the dead which were in them and they were judged every man according to their works. And death and hell were cast into the lake of fire. This is the second death.

And whosoever was not found written in the book of life was cast into the lake of fire. Rev. 20: 11-15

And God shall wipe away all tears from their eyes, and there shall be no more death, neither sorrow, nor crying, neither shall there be any more pain, for the former things are passed away. Rev 21:4

And I saw a new heaven and a new earth for the first heaven and the first earth were passed away and there was no more sea. And I, John, saw the holy city new Jerusalem coming down from God out of heaven, prepared as a bride adorned for her husband. Rev 21:2

And there shall in no wise enter into it anything that defileth, neither whatsoever worketh abomination or maketh a lie, but they which are written in the lamb's book of life. Rev. 21:27

I am the Alpha and Omega, the beginning and the end, the first and the last. Rev. 22:13

Jesus said, *Surely I come quickly."* Amen, even so come Lord Jesus. Rev. 22:20

CPSIA information can be obtained at www.ICGtesting.com
Printed in the USA
BVOW021800081112

305064BV00003B/10/P